E. 504

The Recovery
of Confidence

JOHN W. GARDNER

The Recovery
of Confidence

W·W·Norton & Company·Inc·
NEW YORK

To Jennifer and Gardner and Justine

Contents

Acknowledgments   13

CHAPTER ONE   The Redesign of Institutions   17

     Self-Examination   19
     The Agenda   22
     Problem Solving   23
     Hostility to Institutions   26
     Continuity and Change   31
     Continuous Renewal   33

CHAPTER TWO   Dissent   35

     Defense of the Status Quo   38
     Revolution   42
     The Politics of Provocation   45
     Extremists and the Majority   46
     Violence and Coercion   48
     The Erosion of Confidence   51
     The Endless Interplay   52

CONTENTS

CHAPTER THREE   Society and the Individual   54

Pluralism   54
Internal Communication   58
Release of Individual Potentialities   60
Morale   62

CHAPTER FOUR   Individuality and Community 65

Community   68
Participation   72
The Quality of Life   74
Opportunity to Serve   76
Repair of Fragmentation   78
Self-Discipline   79

CHAPTER FIVE   Leadership and Common
                Purpose   83

The Binding Element in Pluralism   85
Government   88
Public and Private Sectors   91
Leadership   93
Difficulties of Leadership Today   95
Reflection and Action   98

10

CONTENTS

CHAPTER SIX   Self-Contempt and Hope   103

    Expectations and Performance   104
    Criticism Versus Contempt   106
    Dissent and Leadership   108
    The Myth of Regress   112
    Self-Pity and Self-Exoneration   114
    Hope   116

CHAPTER SEVEN   The Renewal of Values   119

    The Internal Gyroscope   120
    The First Step   124
    A Shared Vision   126
    Values in Action   130
    Re-Creating Values   133

CHAPTER EIGHT   We Still Have a Choice   138

    What Can One Man Do?   140
    Tasks for the Tough-Minded   143

APPENDIX   What to Do About the Cities   147

    Money   150
    Governmental Machinery   155

CONTENTS

Patterns of Human Settlement   159
Housing   164
Employment   166
Education   168
Income for the Poor   169
Health   172
Minority Economic Development   173
Law Enforcement and the Administration
  of Justice   175
The Environment   177
Consumer Protection   180
Transportation   182

Index   185

12

Acknowledgments

Over the past year or two a remarkable group of men and women have deepened my understanding of the nation's problems and priorities, and I am indebted to them. They came together after the summer riots of 1967—mayors, minority leaders, businessmen, labor leaders, clergymen, and professional men. They called themselves the Urban Coalition, and in March 1968 they asked me to head their new organization.

The movement has grown steadily, and now involves tens of thousands of men and women in cities large and small throughout the nation. I have visited those men and women in their own communities all over the country. I have worked with them on local and national problems, listened to them, argued with them, and learned from them. This is not a book about the Coalition, but it has been deeply influenced by that experience.

The Coalition addresses itself to the concrete, down-to-earth problems of the city—housing, jobs, education, health, income maintenance, minority economic development, consumer protection, law enforcement, and the administration of justice. But everything the Coalition is trying to do is affected by questions that are not at all concrete. What should our goals be as a nation? Why is it so hard to accomplish social change? Can we design a society capable of continuous renewal? What has happened to our confidence as a people? Can we regain it? It is to these considerations that I address myself.

I am indebted to Professor Don K. Price and to Harvard University for the stimulating assignment that started this book on its way—an invitation to deliver the Godkin Lectures at Harvard in March of 1969. The book is not the Lectures. It contains a great deal of new material, and the material drawn from the Lectures has been completely rewritten. But the Harvard invitation provided the initial stimulus.

My thanks for editorial help go to Helen Rowan, Harold R. Levy, Caryl P. Haskins, and John Corson. For assistance in a thousand other tasks, I'm grateful to my friends Robert Meier, Barbara Collins, John Wood, Wendy Burdsall, Mary Hanson, Sally Roper, and Joyce Follet.

14

The Recovery
of Confidence

CHAPTER ONE

The Redesign
of Institutions

*Many thinking people believe America has seen
its best days.*

—*James Allen (diary entry
for July 26, 1775)*

WE WORRY about the future as we have
never worried before. And we have reason. We see the
brooding threat of nuclear warfare. We know our lakes
are dying, our rivers are growing filthier daily, our atmosphere is becoming increasingly polluted. We are aware of
racial tensions that could tear the nation apart. We understand that oppressive poverty in the midst of affluence is
intolerable. We see that our cities are sliding toward disas-

ter. And these are not problems that stop at our borders. The problems of nuclear warfare, of population, of the environment are impending planetary disasters. We are in trouble as a species.

But it may be that we were in greater peril when we were less worried. We may even be on the mend.

In one of the great passages of Isaiah, the angry Jehovah said, "Make the heart of this people fat!" He intended it as a prelude to desolation, and so it will always be. We were in greater peril in the complacent years, when all of the present evils were in existence or brewing but were layered over by our national smugness.

We will not find a way out of our present troubles until we have the courage to look honestly at evil where evil exists, until we call injustice and dishonor by their right names, and until a large number of Americans from all sectors of opinion—right, left, and center—are willing to acknowledge their own special contribution to our troubles.

Only then will we be ready for the vision of something better. Only then will we be ready for the hard, long, exciting task of building a new America. Only then will we be ready to explore new dimensions of human aspiration and achievement. Only then can we be united again in an inspiring purpose.

When that time comes, we will find it in ourselves to respond. We are capable of so much that is not now asked of us. The courage and endurance are there, poorly hidden beneath our surface pragmatism and frivolity, left somnolent by the moral indifference of modern life, waiting to be called forth when the moment comes. There is no middle road for the spirit. We must call for the best or live with the worst.

In our first century and a half as a nation we were sublimely confident. It doesn't really matter whether it was confidence in the strict sense of the word or simply the buoyancy of the fortunate young. Whatever it was, it is gone. We shall never regain that morning eagerness.

If we are to recover our confidence, it will have to be the confidence of maturity. And it will have to be built, as all mature confidence is built, on a willingness to face problems forthrightly and on some reasonable success in coping with them. That is hard, but adulthood is hard.

SELF-EXAMINATION

There are no easy solutions to the problems we face as a people. There is an almost overpowering temptation to believe that somewhere along the line we made one big mistake, forgot one big truth, overlooked the one key to salvation. We want a simple answer. Seeking such simplicity, ardent but undisciplined minds seize on every new and fashionable nostrum that floats by. But the pat formula will never appear. Many things are wrong. Many things must be done.

Nor can we rest with the one proposition that would receive the endorsement of all Americans today: that the other fellow must mend his ways. Each of us is enormously clever at avoiding self-examination, enormously skilled at self-exoneration. Each of us has some special group on whom to place the blame for our troubles, but the blame must be widely distributed. All of us are somehow implicated.

Among those who must share the burden of guilt are the chiselers, big time and small, who spread the disease of corruption through every level of this society. They cheat on their taxes, they engage in questionable business practices, they make a mockery of professional ethics, they lie to the consumer, they deliver a sloppy job and overcharge for it.

Then there are the men and women who do not really believe in the values that we as Americans have committed ourselves to, the men and women who do not believe in equality of opportunity, in the dignity of the individual, in liberty and justice for all.

There are the extremists, right wing and left wing, with their promise of salvation through violence and coercion. They disguise themselves as saviors, but there is a satanic gleam in their eyes. They believe that hatred will cure and that violence will pave the way to a better world. They do not understand that in her hour of agony, America needs physicians, not executioners.

There are the people of power and influence who could play a significant role in redesigning our institutions but will not do so. Congressional reform is consistently blocked by powerful committee chairmen. Effective legislation for controlling pollution is skillfully emasculated by powerful industrial polluters. University reform has for years been blocked by the most influential faculty members. Tax reform has died a thousand deaths at the hands of vested interests. Union leaders have often slowed the progress of equal job opportunity.

And, finally, there are the "average" citizens who fatten on the yield of this prosperous society but will not turn a hand or make a sacrifice or risk discomfort to help solve its problems. They are earning higher wages or salaries than ever before, buying more consumer goods, enjoying longer and more elaborate vacations—yet they defeat school bond issues, neglect elementary civic duties, allow their local government to fall into disrepair, nurse their prejudices—and complain. And grow fatter. They are angry at the way things are going but they will not help to make them go better. Their apathy is the heaviest burden that this free society must carry.

So the nation moves through a time of supreme danger, her passage made more hazardous by chiselers, by bigots, by extremists, by vested interests, and by the paralyzing lassitude of well-fed citizens. Edmund Burke said, "The effect of liberty to individuals is that they may do what they please. We ought to see what it will please them to do before we risk congratulations."

THE AGENDA

Many Americans are sincerely confused as to where duty lies. Some are confused because they're too lazy to think hard about the problem. Others are confused by the swirl and clash of emotion. And many are confused by the storm of words, slogans and battle cries.

There is a well-tested way out of the dizzying atmosphere of talk and emotion, and that is to put one foot doggedly after another in some concrete, practical activity. And the concrete, practical tasks are there. This is not the place to explore them,* but they can be discovered by anyone who is willing to dig deeply into the agenda before the nation.

That agenda begins with peace. The agenda calls for an end to discrimination. It calls for a relentless attack on poverty. It calls for major reforms in taxation and allocation of resources among federal, state and local lev-

---

* Some are described in the appendix.

22

els. It calls for an end to our shameful tolerance of corruption and decay in state and local government. It calls for new solutions in housing, employment, education, health, pollution control, law enforcement, and the administration of justice.

Historians may record that in the last third of the twentieth century the most important shift in the agenda was the emergence of a concern for man himself and his natural environment. It may be that we are seeing the end of the era in which man ravished his environment, threatening the survival of life on the planet; in which he poisoned himself and the rest of the animate world in the name of profit and progress; in which technological conquests were irresistible, however terrifying the possible biological and human costs. There are signs, faint but hopeful, that we are entering a period that will be characterized by a deeper respect for the natural world, a deeper awareness of our oneness with nature, a recognition that our fate as individuals is inseparable from our fate as a species and the future of life on this planet.

PROBLEM SOLVING

Why have we had such difficulty—steadily mounting difficulty—in getting at our problems? One

23

might blame our apathy, or our unwillingness to spend, or our failure to understand the problems, or our resistance to change. But something else is wrong, something central, something crucial. As we examine the intensive and multitudinous efforts to cope with the problems, we are driven to a significant conclusion: there are some things that are gravely wrong with our society as a problem-solving mechanism. The machinery is not working in a fashion that will permit us to solve any of our problems effectively.

That reality is supremely boring to most social critics. They are deeply reluctant to think about the complex and technical processes by which the society functions. And in the end their unwillingness to grapple with those processes defeats them.

One of the reasons people interested in improving conditions never quite come to grips with this central issue is that they are preoccupied with specific evils that must be corrected. I don't blame them. But the result is that each reformer comes to his task with a little bundle of desired changes. The implication is that if appropriate reforms are carried through and the defects corrected, the society will be wholly satisfactory and the work of the reformer done.

That is a primitive way of viewing social change. We are creating new problems as rapidly as we solve the old.

The crucial task is to design a society (and institutions) capable of continuous change, continuous renewal, continuous responsiveness.

We must dispose of the notion that social change is a process that alters a tranquil status quo. Today there is no tranquillity to alter. Given the swift transformations in our world, even institutions that are fairly young, as history goes, find themselves woefully out of date. The rush of change brings a kind of instant antiquity.

A first step toward a sound philosophy of social renewal* would be to break our habit of concentrating exclusively on routine repair activities. The mechanic faced with a defective carburetor can put it back in working order and stop there. Or, if he is a very gifted mechanic, he may sit down and design an improved unit, less subject to breakdown. If he is still more imaginative, he may think of a whole new means, simpler and more efficient, for mixing air and fuel in the proper proportions for combustion.

This is not to say that we must be infatuated with everything new and reject everything old. We have seen change that does senseless damage to significant

* I have discussed the processes of growth, decay, and renewal as they exhibit themselves in societies, institutions and individual lives in my book *Self-Renewal* (New York: Harper & Row, 1964).

continuities—natural neighborhoods destroyed by the highway bulldozer, historic landmarks razed to make way for commercial development.

In all growth there is a complex interweaving of continuity and change. One purpose of social change is to find new solutions that will preserve old values. When the spring dries up the farmer seeks a new source of water, not for love of novelty but to bring himself back into balance with his environment.

HOSTILITY TO INSTITUTIONS

Unfortunately, all social effort today is complicated by the hostility men feel toward their social institutions. We must try to understand that hostility.

From the beginning, men had believed that all the major features of their lives were determined by immemorial custom or fate or the will of God. Then in the seventeenth and eighteenth centuries increasing numbers of people began to believe that men could shape their own institutions and gain command of the social forces that buffeted them.

No one knows all the ingredients that produced the change, but we can identify some major elements. One was the emergence, with the Scientific Revolution, of a way of thinking that sought objective cause-and-effect relationships. People trained to think that way about the physical world were bound to note that the social world too had its causes and effects—and bound to imagine, sooner or later, that one might manipulate the cause to alter the effect.

At the same time people were less and less inclined to explain their daily lives and institutions in terms of God's will. And that trend has continued to this day. Less and less do men suppose, even those who believe devoutly in a supreme being, that God busies himself with detailed, day-to-day administration of the world.

Meanwhile, with new modes of transportation and communication men discovered that human institutions varied enormously from one society to the next. It became increasingly difficult to think of one's own institutions as unalterable, increasingly easy to conceive of a society in which men consciously shaped their institutions and customs.

The result is that today any bright high school student can talk easily about social forces and institutional change. A few centuries ago, even for learned men such matters were ordained, not subject to analysis, fixed in the great design of things.

Up to a point the newer views were immensely exhilarating. In the writings of our Founding Fathers one encounters a mood approaching exaltation as they proceeded to shape a new nation. But more recently another consequence has become apparent. The new view that man can shape his institutions turns out to place an enormous burden on the social structures he has evolved over the centuries. Those structures have become the sole target and receptacle for all of man's hostility and hope. He has replaced his fervent prayer to God with a shrill cry of anger against his own institutions.

Men can tolerate extraordinary hardship if they think it is an unalterable part of life's travail. But their tempers have a short fuse when hardship results from the decision of another human being, presumably no better than themselves. An administered frustration, unsanctioned by religion or custom or deeply rooted values, is more than the spirit can bear.

But that is the lot of contemporary man. It is an administered age. So increasingly men rage at their institutions. All kinds of men rage at all kinds of institutions, here and around the world.

Yet the past three centuries have seen a vast and impressive movement in the direction of institutions that are responsive to the will of men. There have been setbacks, to be sure, and trouble and hypocrisy and failure —but over the years the trend has been unmistakable. Why, then, in the late twentieth century, have men turned on their institutions as if to destroy them in a fit of impatience?

Clearly, it has something to do with the sharp rise in human expectations that has occurred throughout the world. Men have come to demand more and more of their institutions, and with greater intransigence.

What people aspire to is not unreasonable. They want food, housing, jobs, security, dignity—hardly an irresponsible list. But the time scale on which they want these things—now!—poses great difficulties. The demands for instant performance lead to instant disillusionment, for while aspirations leap ahead, human institutions remain sluggish—less sluggish to be sure than at any previous time in history, but still inadequately responsive to human need.

So the stage is set for the most familiar confrontation of modern life—between people who demand change and institutions that resist it. The institutions alter, but never fast enough, and those who seek change are bitterly disappointed.

In the resulting conflict we find our institutions caught in a savage crossfire between uncritical lovers and unloving critics. On the one side, those who love their institutions tend to smother them in an embrace of death, loving their rigidities more than their promise, shielding them from life-giving criticism. On the other side there

29

has arisen a breed of critics without love, skilled in demolition but untutored in the arts by which human institutions are nurtured and strengthened and made to flourish.

Where human institutions are concerned, love without criticism brings stagnation, and criticism without love brings destruction. The swifter the pace of change, the more lovingly men must care for and criticize their institutions to keep them intact through the turbulent passages.

Accompanying the hostility to established institutions is a breakdown in authority, in just about every dimension: the authority of parents, religion, custom, social class, the law, and the state. Not only has authority been eroded; critics have developed extraordinarily effective techniques for cutting public figures down to size. The politics of derision turns out to be devastatingly effective, and—in an unhealthy way—downright fun. No one who has reviewed the sweep of American history will believe that our leaders and public figures—at every level of public life—are any more deficient in quality than they were a decade or a century ago. That they seem so is due partly to the breakdown in authority and partly to our increased skill in stripping them of dignity. Men in power have never been fully protected by the mantle of respect surrounding high office, but today they are naked as jaybirds.

These attitudes and conditions—the hostility to institutions, the expectation-despair syndrome, the erosion of authority—create the climate within which the nation sets its goals, appraises its capacity to achieve those goals, and moves toward their fulfillment. It is unfortunately a climate of nay-saying, a climate that not only fosters corrosive appraisals of our society and our leaders but pits us against one another in frustration and anger.

CONTINUITY AND CHANGE

All of this suggests that we can less and less afford to limit ourselves to routine repair of breakdowns in our institutions. We see in all clarity that many of our institutions are ill fitted to cope with the tasks the modern world presses on them. Yet we find those institutions apparently incapable of change, even in the face of attacks by those who would destroy them altogether. Unless we are willing to see a final confrontation between institutions that refuse to change and critics bent on destruction, we had better get on with the task of redesigning our society.

Such redesign is not new to us. In our history as a nation we have done a great deal of social inventing and innovating. Among the consequences are the land-grant college, the county agent, antitrust legislation, the Federal Reserve system, the Social Security system.

A new approach to the redesign of institutions should be of particular interest to liberals at this moment in history, for repair of the liberal tradition is itself a matter of urgent importance. There is much about that tradition as it has evolved over the past thirty-five years in this country that we must honor and preserve—its hopefulness about man and society, its generosity of spirit, its concern for human need, its willingness to re-examine (and if necessary revise) the status quo in the service of evolutionary growth. But liberalism does not, at this point, need pious defenders. It needs a new approach. It needs to shed some outworn postures and quirks and adopt a modern strategy of social renewal.

Liberals have two paths open to them, one easy and catastrophic, the other difficult and regenerative. The easy path is to live on the clichés and stereotypes of the past thirty-five years, to be nostalgic about once-bright heroes and hopes, to live in an old attic of outworn ideas and antagonisms. The hard path is to formulate a new way of conceiving the problem of social change, a new way of thinking about the tasks ahead.

32

CONTINUOUS RENEWAL

There are many ways in which a nation can die. It can die of internal strife, tearing itself apart. It can die of indifference, of an unwillingness to face its problems, an incapacity to respond to the suffering of its people. Or a nation can die of old age, not chronological so much as psychological old age—a waning of energy, an incapacity to learn new ways.

There is no likelihood that we will fail to respond to the sweep of change. It forces our hand. The danger is that we will respond sluggishly. The danger is the creeping disaster that overtakes a society which little by little loses a commanding grip on its problems and its future.

Our society is not unusually resistant to change. But we do not have to look far to identify signs of age and rigidity in our institutions. The departments of the federal government are in grave need of renewal; state government is in most places a nineteenth-century relic; in most cities, municipal government is a waxwork of stiffly preserved anachronisms; the system of taxation is a tangle of dysfunctional measures; the courts are crippled by archaic organizational arrangements; the unions, the professions, the universities, the corporations—each has spun its own impenetrable web of vested interests.

Make no mistake about the evil consequences of those rigidities. They are to blame for the paradox of abject poverty in the world's richest nation, for the fact that millions of citizens of that nation live in substandard housing, for scandalous inequities in school finance, for gross failures in the administration of justice, for the fact that health services are virtually unavailable to many of the poor.

But to blame such evils on institutional rigidity does not trace the trouble to its source. The rigidities are supported by solid citizens who strive to be virtuous but dislike change—and never, never fail to protect that part of the system that guards their own selfish interests.

That human institutions require periodic redesign, if only because of their tendency to decay, is not a minor fact about them, nor easily overlooked. Taking the whole span of history, there is no more important lesson to be learned.

How curious, then, that in all of history, with all the immensely varied principles on which societies have been designed and operated, no people has seriously attempted to take into account the aging of institutions and to provide for their continuous renewal. Why shouldn't we be the first to do so?

34

CHAPTER TWO

Dissent

*Those societies which cannot combine reverence
to their symbols with freedom of revision must
ultimately decay either from anarchy or from the
slow atrophy of a life stifled by useless shadows.*

—Alfred North Whitehead

IN UNDERTAKING the redesign of our institutions, it is necessary to ask what kind of society we want.

We are all familiar with the young radicals who reject the world as it is but can't specify the kind of world they want. The truth is that most middle-of-the-road and conservative citizens are equally unprepared to specify the kind of society we should be striving to achieve.

It is child's play to mount a devastating critique of the

existing system—any existing system. It is child's play to have unquestioning faith in the existing system. The hard task is to specify appropriate directions of change.

We must face that hard task. We cannot stand still. We cannot go back. The forces of change are altering our society whether we like it or not. We are moving on to something new. If we are to have any influence on the course of events, we must have some conception of what we would like that new thing to be. Among other things, it must be a society capable of continuous renewal.

What would be the attributes of such a society?

Let us begin with the most controversial attribute. The society capable of renewal will provide for dissent, for the emergence of alternatives to official doctrine or widely accepted assumptions. It will provide for honest appraisal of the disparity between widely professed ideals and existing conditions.

It is not just the national government or the Establishment (whatever that is) that can profit from criticism. Corporations, universities, churches, professions, government agencies—all must foster a climate in which assumptions may be questioned and settled policies challenged. We are beginning to understand that there are innumerable Establishments, many of them hardly recognizable in traditional terms. In the absence of criticism, every organization ends up being managed for the benefit of the people who run it: most schools tend to be run in such a way as to serve the purposes of the teachers; the Navy tends to be run for the benefit of naval officers; the vested interests of postal employees are the predominant factor in controlling and directing the future of the post office; the policies and practices of most universities are explicable chiefly in terms of the vested interests of the professors.

Critics who are so preoccupied with the fantasy of a single all-powerful Establishment that they ignore these facts are missing one of the most significant features of the contemporary scene.

Our society rates very high in sheer volume of expressed dissent. But much of it is fruitless. We can and must construct more effective means of criticizing the institutions and processes of our society. We have plenty of generalized caterwauling about society's faults. We need more specific, on-target criticism. For a variety of reasons, it is hard to come by.

It is easy to approve of dissent in the abstract, but often difficult in real life. The most visible dissenters are too aggressive for comfort. They carry an unwelcome message. They promise inconvenience, altercations, embarrassment. And inevitably mingled among them are the fools, neurotics, and self-aggrandizers that one finds in any segment of the population.

37

In short, the task of remaining open to dissent isn't just a matter of listening tolerantly, congratulating oneself all the while for exemplary open-mindedness. It is apt to be an annoying experience. But it is worth the trouble.

DEFENSE OF THE STATUS QUO

All institutions, religious or commercial, political or educational, are extremely skillful in protecting themselves from the proddings of dissent.

The most impenetrable defense is deafness—not anger, not indignation, not punishment, just inability to hear. Such functional deafness is familiar to every corporate executive or government official who has tried to force a re-examination of accepted policies. Conservationists working in the first half of the twentieth century faced innumerable obstacles, but none more discouraging than the sheer incapacity of most Americans to hear what they were saying. We hear them now but the hour is late. Students of state and local government tried to alert us several decades ago to the ailments and anomalies of the governing processes at that level. We didn't exile them or suppress them—we just didn't listen.

More familiar among the defenses against dissent are

all the various forms of punishment inflicted on the dissenter. Curiously, the idea of dissent has become so respectable that rarely does anyone punish a man just because he disagrees. The disagreement must first be identified as something worse—disloyalty, "unsoundness," or a penchant for troublemaking. What follows may not be punishment in the formal sense so much as exclusion. The executive who dissents may simply find that he is less and less a member of the inner circle of management. The conservative economist applying for a post in a liberal university department may find that his application just never comes to the top of the pile.

Rarely, however, do protectors of the status quo limit themselves to such low-keyed methods. They are more likely to strive for highly visible sanctions that will not only dispose of the offender but strike fear in the hearts of others who hold similar views.

Another powerful defense against the dissenter is to deny him the information on which criticism might be based. Information is the lifeblood of effective dissent. Government agencies and business corporations treat a good deal of information as privileged not out of necessity but out of a primitive (and sound) instinct that what a potential critic doesn't know can't be used to indict them. Every serious critic will sooner or later find himself fighting the battle of information.

But formal secrecy is a little old-fashioned as a means of concealment. For the modern defender of the status quo the functional equivalent of secrecy is complexity. Contemporary organizational processes are so intricate that decisions and their consequences are virtually invisible except to a knowing few. The defense is almost impenetrable, and the only thing decision-makers need do to remain protected is to avoid any move toward clarification.

In the face of such obstacles, there are a variety of things we must do if we wish to foster a healthy tradition of dissent.

First, we must generate a greater volume of technically expert, knowing dissent on many of the highly complex matters that affect our lives—fiscal policy, military expenditures, income maintenance, nuclear energy, and so on. Such criticism requires men and women who have observed at close range (as participants, consultants or journalists) the intricate processes in question but who have an outside base from which objective comment is possible. Every aspect of our national life needs the attention of such highly expert, inside-outside critics.

Second, we must build into organizations, particularly in government, the evaluative processes that will permit us to judge performance. This means that government officials must be required to be specific about goals—

that is, about outcomes that would have to be achieved to count a given activity successful; they must develop measures to determine whether those outcomes have occurred; and they must apply the measures systematically to performance—all to the end that they can say of any program, "It worked" or "It didn't work." Institutional processes can never be wholly caught in the net of systematic assessment, but there is no excuse for our present slovenliness about evaluation.

Third, we need to develop complaint and appeal procedures that will permit the clientele of any institution to seek redress of grievances.

We are not without channels for complaint and grievance today. The courts are a means of seeking redress. With respect to federal departments, members of Congress are often effective ombudsmen for their constituents. The newspapers provide a channel for some grievances (it is common in Washington for a cabinet member to learn of some malfunction in his own department by reading the papers). But all these channels tend to be limited to complainants who are affluent, influential, or moderately sophisticated—or have a spectacular complaint to lodge. The ordinary citizen with an ordinary complaint nurses his anger.

What is at stake is the responsiveness and accountability of government at every level and of institutions in the private sector as well. Popular interest in the idea of an ombudsman attests to the need felt by the average citizen. He can't understand his utilities bill. He writes to the Internal Revenue Service about a tax refund and finds he is corresponding with a computer. He begins to believe there is no way to penetrate the monstrous institutions that govern his life.

But the ombudsman idea in its popular form—the notion of an independent high official with an honest face and a big mail box—is an oversimplification of the need. We must build into every institution orderly procedures for the hearing and redress of grievances.

Such procedures benefit not only the client but the institution complained against. Every organization filters the feedback on performance to screen out information it doesn't want to face up to. Effective complaint procedures can cut through that self-serving filter mechanism.

REVOLUTION

There are some dissenters who say, "We don't need reform, we need revolution. The whole system is rotten and should be destroyed." Of course, many who say it don't really mean it. There is an awesome theatricality about today's radicalism, and the apocalyptic assertion is much in vogue. If one patiently questions people who make such statements, not attacking them but exploring their views, one uncovers a variety of conventional radical positions, most of which have been around for a generation or more and have survived peaceably (if not necessarily comfortably) within our traditional political structure.

But, of course, some who call for destruction of the system really mean it. At first, one is puzzled by their failure to understand that when a social system is destroyed, the resulting chaos is supremely antagonistic to *any* organized purposes, including the purposes of those who initiated the destruction; and by their failure to understand that periods of chaos are followed by periods of iron rule.

Those who seek to bring societies down always dream that after the blood bath *they* will be calling the tune. But after the chaos no one knows what kind of dictator would emerge. Since physical force would probably reign supreme, the rulers would presumably be those most skilled in the use of weapons—in other words, the police and the military services. So we are asked to destroy the system, suffer the resulting chaos, put ourselves in the hands of the steel-hard inheritors of chaos, go through the long rebuilding process—all with no assurance whatever of a better outcome (or even as

43

good an outcome). The proposal dissolves under examination.

Some of today's revolutionaries, particularly younger ones, have fallen victim to an old and naïve doctrine—that man is naturally good, humane, decent, just, and honorable, but that corrupt and wicked institutions have transformed the noble savage into a civilized monster. Destroy the corrupt institutions, they say, and man's native goodness will flower. There isn't anything in history or anthropology to confirm the thesis, but it has survived down the generations.

Of course, the assertion that society's ills are incurable often masks purposes shallower than revolution. Since the assertion cannot be proven wrong, it lends itself to those whose chief interest is in the theatricalities of debate. And since it makes remedial efforts pointless, it serves those who through laziness or impatience have no intention of mastering the processes of social change.

Although left-wing revolutionaries have managed to get most of the attention lately, we are in just as much danger from extremism of the right, from all those in our society who live with their finger on the trigger of repressive action—leaders who make political capital out of fear and anger, law-enforcement officers who are seeking an excuse for harsh measures, and all the secret militiamen who lurk in the shadows of our national life. The extreme right is fully as radical in its intentions as the extreme left. Though it mouths the pieties of flag and constitution, it would—given the opportunity—fashion a society that would be utterly unrecognizable to the authors of the Bill of Rights.

THE POLITICS OF PROVOCATION

For the person who concludes that the system is wholly evil and must be destroyed, the end justifies the means; he opposes measures that would diminish suffering now because they blunt the revolutionary mood. The majority must be manipulated for its own good (as he defines it). He has no interest in rational examination of issues; indeed, he will deliberately confuse issues or block communication in an effort to prevent such examination —for example, by preventing opponents from being heard. He will devise traps to demean those in authority, destroying their dignity where possible. He will exploit the mass media, feeding their hunger for excitement and conflict.

He will plan deliberately provocative confrontations designed to lead officials to "overreact," knowing that if they do it will bring to his side naïve sympathizers who hate to see officials act repressively. And if officials "un-

45

derreact" or seem to doubt their own legitimacy, that too favors the revolutionary. If those in authority were perfectly wise, such tactics would never work. But officials are human, subject to fatigue and not immune to error. If the provocateurs are persistent enough and ingenious enough, they can sooner or later trap any official into unwise action.

Whether of the left wing or the right, the stock in trade of the extremist is rage and hatred—and there's always a market for what he has to sell. It's fun to get mad and it's fun to hate. Simple-minded people indulge such emotions without dissembling, and are duly criticized. More guileful people discovered long ago that the big psychic payoff comes in finding an apparently noble cause in which to indulge one's rage and hatred. Then one can draw dividends from both sides of the transaction, satisfying both the new morality and the old Adam.

It would be comforting to believe that only extremists traffic in the destructive emotions, but one can identify a fair number of "respectable" leaders who make a regular practice of exploiting fear and prejudice and anger.

EXTREMISTS AND THE MAJORITY

For a long time we have preserved the fiction that the drama of social change is a conflict between dissenters and the top layers of the Establishment. But as the most impatient of our critics fling themselves in kamikaze assaults on sluggish institutions, they eventually come into head-on collision with the people who are most deeply implicated in the sluggishness, namely, the great majority. The stone wall against which many reforms shatter is the indifference, or downright hostility, of that majority.

The collision between angry dissenters and lower-middle-class opponents is exceedingly dangerous. As long as the dissenters are confronting the top layers of the power structure they are dealing with people who are reasonably secure, often willing to compromise, able to yield ground without anxiety. But when the dissenters collide with the lower middle class they confront an insecure opponent, quick to anger and not prepared to yield an inch.

It is at this point that young rebels find great appeal in Herbert Marcuse's ideas. When they think they are attacking the fat cats at the top of the social structure, democratic doctrine seems a serviceable banner to wrap themselves in. But democratic doctrine suddenly becomes a considerable embarrassment when they discover that "the people" they seek to liberate are in fact bitterly opposed to them.

Marcuse deals with that difficulty by saying that democracy and tolerance are themselves barriers to the overthrow of an evil society. He favors a more "directed" society. In doing so, he makes the assumption made by all who fall into authoritarian doctrines—that, in the directed society he advocates, people who share his values will be calling the tune. So thought the businessmen who supported Hitler.

It would be wrong to leave the impression that the great majority of "middle Americans" are a stubbornly conservative force. They may react angrily against violence and extremism, but they have shown on many occasions that under vigorous and imaginative leadership they will support forward-looking policies.

VIOLENCE AND COERCION

Along with, but not necessarily linked to, revolutionary ideologies we have seen the swift rise of violence and coercion as instruments of social protest. It is easy to divert oneself with subtle justifications of violence; it is more to the point to reflect on its stark consequences. Violence evokes—even seeks—a violent answer. Coercion invites countercoercion. The student with an inclination toward violent or coercive action and the policeman with a taste for brutality are waiting for each other. The politician with a fondness for repressive measures and the ghetto leader with a leaning toward violence

48

are seeking each other—and eventually they find each other. Each reacting to the other, they escalate first the tensions and then the overt acts, and draw increasing numbers of moderates into the deadly interplay. Thus do they weave their own shrouds and ours too.

One hears a special justification for violence in the case of the ghetto riots. The riots were necessary, it was argued, to produce fear in the power structure and thereby to get action on the social front.

It is true that the riots provoked fear, but there were many consequences besides constructive social action. The riots led many Americans, including members of Congress, to resist or oppose further federal programs for the cities. The riots led both police and citizens to arm themselves and led to a heavy vote for political candidates not sympathetic to the concerns of the ghetto.

To cite only the favorable consequences of the riots and ignore the unfavorable is disastrously near-sighted. The provoking of fear is a dangerous form of brinksmanship. It may bring constructive results or it may unleash emotions that will lead to the suppression of all freedom.

It is an old failing of the intellectual that he has fantasies of a rather genteel revolution in which the revolutionaries stir up just enough turmoil to make comfortable people thoroughly uncomfortable. But one cannot have revolution in carefully measured doses. Events will not be kind to those who unleash the furies of human emotion in the service of their own carefully calculated goals. Emotions get out of hand. No one knows what climax they will build toward, nor who will get hurt, nor what the end will be. Anyone who unleashes man's destructive impulses had better stand a long way back.

Violence begets violence. Hatred feeds on hatred. No society can risk repeated internecine strife. Even if the conflict finally stabilizes, it may leave deep, permanent lines of division.

Some generous-minded people argue that the only proper response to citizen violence is renewed determination to correct the social injustices that so often lie behind it. It is a half truth. One must act with all possible energy to combat injustice and *at the same time* oppose violence.

The anarchist paves the way for the authoritarian. Either we will have a civil order in which discipline is internalized in the breast of each free and responsible citizen or we will see repressive measures designed to re-establish order. Everyone who cares about freedom will pray for the former and avoid courses of action that lead to the latter.

Typically, the re-establishment of order after anarchy is accomplished with the approval of the people even though repressive measures are involved. After rampant disorder they want order even at a price. Unfortunately, they can rarely judge the price.

More sinister in every way than the violence of citizens is illegal violence on the part of authorities. When police or National Guard troops break the well-established disciplines of the law-enforcement officer and give way to vindictiveness, racism, and brutality, the state suffers a terrible wound.

THE EROSION OF CONFIDENCE

All who contribute to an atmosphere of violence, all who foster (or seek to exploit) hatred and rage, all who set us one against another in the furtherance of their own purposes—whether they are politicians or students or blacks or policemen or writers—are inflicting grave damage on the society.

Let us not overdramatize the possibilities of wrecking the system. Such people cannot bring the society down in the sense of instant or even rapid demolition. But they can loosen the cement that holds the society together. They can set us against one another, obscure the issues, and diminish to a fatal degree the confidence, morale, and conviction that enable a people to face and surmount its problems. Confused and divided, doubting

51

ourselves, we could drift deeper and deeper into disorder, mutual distrust, anger, fear and hatred.

Human institutions are vulnerable, and free institutions are particularly vulnerable because they must allow
wide latitude for dissent, even destructive dissent.

Our notions of the downfall of a civilization stem
from the fall of Rome—barbarian hordes attacking from
without, a breakdown of morals within. But those are
consequences. The event is less visible. It involves an erosion of shared commitment and an erosion of confidence.

THE ENDLESS INTERPLAY

Anyone who has watched the endless interac-
tion of dissent, defense of the status quo, radicalism and
reaction, competition for the mind of the "average" citizen, manipulation by politicians of the tensions inherent
in change—anyone who has watched all of that over the
years must experience feelings that mingle fascination,
boredom, amusement and despair. Defenders of the status quo seek to identify dissent with disloyalty. Dissenters
grow more shrill as they become more frustrated. If the
far right overreaches itself, as in the Joseph McCarthy
era, the majority moves away from them. If the far left

overreaches itself, as in some of the riots and rantings of the late 1960's, the majority moves away from *them*.

Meanwhile, unprincipled leaders engage in the sad and dirty business of exploiting for their own advantage the angers and fears of the people.

Those seriously interested in the health-giving processes of dissent must devise new ways to cut through the formidable defenses of the status quo. And at the same time they must discourage self-defeating forms of dissent that lessen the possibility of beneficent change.

CHAPTER THREE

Society and the Individual

The poet does not write chiefly for his own generation; he must therefore write about permanent things, or things that are . . . perpetually renewed, like grass and humanity.

—*Robinson Jeffers*

Wᴴᴬᵀ WOULD BE some of the other attributes of a society capable of continuous renewal?

PLURALISM

It would be characterized by a productive balance (perhaps tension is a better word) between pluralism and a concern for the shared purposes of all segments of society. Pluralism without a concern for common purposes moves toward chaos and the anarchic play of vested interest. A concern for common purposes without pluralism leads to totalitarian solutions.

I shall discuss pluralism here, and the balancing elements of common purpose at other points throughout the book. We mean by pluralism a society characterized by variety, by choices, by alternatives, and by multiple foci of power and initiative. We have just such pluralism in this society today. But it would be folly to ignore that the logic of modern large-scale organization, governmental or corporate, tends to squeeze out pluralism and to move toward one comprehensive system of power. We must work against that trend. In our own society this requires, in practical terms, a concern for the vitality of local leadership, for the strength and autonomy of state and local government, for the vigor and creativity of the private sector.

There are those, of course, who assert that our pluralism is illusory and that in fact the nation is ruled by a monolithic power—the military-industrial complex, or an "Establishment." That there is a military-industrial complex no one can doubt. That it wields considerable power is irrefutable. But it is not a cohesive force, and it is powerful only with respect to circumscribed issues.

55

To exaggerate its role is to ignore (and spare from public scrutiny) many other forces that are potent in shaping public policy—farmers, highway contractors, the extractive industries, junior colleges, land-grant colleges, real estate interests, mayors, postal employees, governors, savings and loan companies, unions, the aged, the highly competent lobbies run by professional groups (doctors, educators) and so on. I have observed them all in action and I can attest to their effectiveness.

The sheer multiplicity of vested interests makes the concept of an Establishment wholly unrealistic at the national level. It is not unrealistic at the local level. In the typical small city there is a fairly coherent group of people who "run" the life of the city. But it is much less true of large cities, and wholly untrue of the nation. Anyone who has seen at close range (and participated in) the intense and disorderly clash of interests out of which national policy is forged knows that at that level power is extremely fragmented.

Nationally, the concept of an Establishment survives because it is the backbone of cocktail-party sociology. It is a boon to people who haven't done their homework and don't really know who holds decisive power on what issues.

We do have a pluralistic system today. But the forces at work to diminish pluralism are observable in both public and private spheres. If they proceed unchecked in the public sphere there will soon, say in twenty-five years, be no such thing as state, county, and city government. There will be one all-encompassing governmental system.

As the trend proceeds in the private sphere, corporations merge, newspapers merge, small colleges and small businesses find survival increasingly difficult. In neither public nor private spheres is the trend ideologically determined. It is simply in the nature of modern social organization to evolve in that direction.

Most young people today seem to sense that trend and, without being very analytical about it, oppose it. They tend to be decentralist, hostile to hierarchical organization, suspicious of large agglomerations of power. They are highly critical of the federal government, indeed of all government. They are just as hostile to big business, of course, and occasionally one hears the view expressed that private enterprise should be abolished. It may not have occurred to the proponents of such a view that abolition of private enterprise would mean a vast expansion of government. General Motors would not disappear. It would simply be lumped with Ford, Chrysler, Boeing, Pan American, and so on in an unimaginably vast Ministry of Transportation.

If we are to retain pluralism we are going to have to

57

work consciously toward that end. We are going to have to understand the ways in which government and the private sector can assort their functions, each enhancing the vitality of the other. And we are going to have to untangle the mutually frustrating relationships of federal, state, and local governments.

A more difficult problem in the long run is the preservation—or creation—of some measure of pluralism in life styles. Mass merchandising, the mass media and the logic of large-scale organization make for standardization—of dress, language, ideas and home decoration. We must encourage pluralism in those dimensions too.

INTERNAL COMMUNICATION

The advantages of pluralism are diminished if the various elements of the society are out of touch with one another. A society that is capable of continuous renewal will have effective internal communication among its diverse elements. We do not have that today. We are drowning in a torrent of talk, but most of it serves only to raise the noise level. Grave gaps in communication exist between the businessman and the working man, between white and black, between young and old, between conservative and liberal, between public and private sectors. They do not engage in the open and constructive dialogue that would permit each to understand the other's values. Communication in a healthy society must be more than a flow of messages; it must be a means of conflict resolution, a means of cutting through the rigidities that divide and paralyze a community.

The society capable of continuous renewal will have more varied and effective means of conflict resolution than we have today. We are witnessing a polarization of groups, and we have seen the steady refinement of techniques for producing that polarization. In such a time, all the gaps in communication that characterize our fragmented society become dangerous, and one group's ignorance of another easily leads on to fear and hostility.

It is only in the past fifteen or twenty years that anyone has worked systematically and analytically on the problem of resolving human conflicts. And we have learned a great deal—far more than we have ever applied. It is not the fact of conflict itself that is threatening. In a free society there will always be tumult as groups with conflicting purposes collide. That is part of the great design. What endangers a society are the consequences of violent, prolonged and savage conflict— deeply embedded hatreds, devastating breakdowns in communication, and the rigidity of entrenched defensive

59

positions.

And it is not only internally that a society must pursue the path of peace. In the world at large the task will be even harder—and we have even more to learn about it.

RELEASE OF INDIVIDUAL POTENTIALITIES

All discussions of the vitality of societies and institutions must eventually come back to the individual.

The society capable of continuous renewal will be one that develops to the full its human resources, that removes obstacles to individual fulfillment.* In these matters our record is uneven—good in some respects, shameful in others. In education, in the biomedical sciences, and in a number of other fields we have worked hard and accomplished much to combat the conditions that stunt human growth and thwart individual promise. But our black citizens and some other minorities have struggled under socially imposed handicaps profoundly incompatible with our ideals.

Some believe that the race issue has been overempha-

* I have examined the process by which a society seeks, develops, and uses individual talent in my book *Excellence* (New York: Harper, 1960).

sized recently. It hasn't. Slavery was the heaviest burden the national conscience has ever borne. The burden was thrown off in a bloody war. But inequality remained, inequality that mocked the most ardent professions of the American ideal.

To bring full justice and equality to black people is the historic assignment of this generation. We cannot evade that assignment and preserve the kind of nation we care about. The commonly repeated expressions of our national ideal say that every individual is of value. Our past record of dealing with black Americans says something very different. A reckoning was bound to come, and it has come in this generation. It will not be resolved by violence or hatred or bitterness or police suppression. It will be resolved only by patient, determined efforts on the part of the great, politically moderate majority of whites and blacks, strengthened by leaders of courage who refuse to indulge in popular appeals to fear and prejudice.

After a decade of unprecedented activity in pursuing the goal of equal opportunity, we know very well the agenda before us: vigorous renewal of the attack on poverty, intensified civil rights enforcement, heavier aid to education in low-income areas, improved delivery of health services to the poor, more equitable administration of justice, housing, jobs, and a new approach to income maintenance. The faster we get on with that agenda the better.

The concern for individual fulfillment extends far beyond questions of race, of course. It is central to all aspects of education and to many aspects of employment. And if we are serious about individual fulfillment we shall also give attention to the more subtle threats to psychic wholeness inherent in the fragmentation of work, the disappearance of community, the split between intellect and emotion.

MORALE

A high level of morale is essential for the arduous tasks of renewal. Citizens must have faith in the possibility of achieving their shared goals.

The diminished morale in this nation in recent years stems from a great many factors—the severity of internal conflict, a failure of leadership, a detested war, the incapacity of the society to solve grave and obvious problems, a visible disparity between the values we profess and the practices we tolerate—but more than anything else contemporary demoralization stems from a breakdown in the relationship of the individual to society.

That breakdown is not visible to the naked eye, and

its consequences come to the surface slowly. But it is a supremely dangerous condition, and it is implicated in many of today's social ills, from apathy to violence, from drug abuse to juvenile crime. It is widely assumed that the condition applies only to those whose opinions or style of dress advertise their alienation, but it may be found, in some degree, throughout the population, among employees of corporate empires and government agencies, among young professionals and suburban housewives.

Consider some of the more familiar symptoms as the individual experiences them. He may feel powerless and useless in a vast and complex society. He may suffer from loss of a sense of belonging, of meaning, of "connection." Sometimes he feels the society has deprived him of his identity and turned him into a number. Such feelings may lead to apathy and passivity, or to alienation and all the various forms of dropping out.

The symptoms may be found in some measure throughout the society. If one defines the term "dropout" to mean a person who has given up serious effort to meet his responsibilities, then every business office, government agency, golf club, and university faculty would yield its quota.

Let us admit at the start that we do not fully understand these feelings on the part of the individual. Consider the feeling of powerlessness. We complain that in

63

this complex world we can't control our own fate, can't control our own institutions; but rarely if ever in history have individuals had much control over their institutions or their lives. It is sentimental to suppose that in simpler times men had more choices or greater control. We complain that we don't understand what's going on. But the average man has never understood more, and with greater sophistication, than he understands today.

So why do we feel so frustrated? Have our aspirations for understanding and control of our lives risen? Or was it less frustrating when we thought that our lives were in the grip of forces essentially unreachable (Fate, God, Tradition, the King) in contrast to the present conviction that our lives are in the hands of reachable and highly vulnerable men (the Mayor)?

Or is it the enigmatic quality of our situation that upsets us? When we believed that the king or the courthouse gang were in charge, at least we weren't puzzled. Perhaps the most frustrating thing of all is not to know whom to blame.

Despite many uncertainties concerning the roots of the trouble, there is a great deal we can do—and do now—to repair the breakdown in the relationship between the individual and society. In the following chapter I shall examine some of the possibilities.

CHAPTER FOUR

Individuality and Community

> *Individuality is something to be built for the sake
> of something else. It is a structure of potential en-
> ergies for expenditure in the service of an idea, a
> cultural endeavor, the betterment of man, an
> emergent value.*
>
> —*H. A. Murray*

IT IS a significant attribute of human social
systems, as compared with other kinds of systems, that
each individual (that is, each element in the system) has
extensive power to function on his own, to initiate, to re-
direct his own activities. Such is the potentiality of the
individual.

But the self-directive attributes of the individual are not irrepressible. The evidence of history and anthropology is clear on that point. Individual initiative appears to be rather easily extinguished. And the spark, once smothered in a society, may stay out for centuries.

No society that cares about its own vitality will permit that to happen. A society (or organization) that deadens the individual cuts off its own sources of renewal and cements over the seedbed of its future growth. And that, briefly, is the danger facing any large, intricately organized society. Unfortunately, the end toward which all modern societies seem to be moving, whatever their ideology, is the beehive model. The total system perfects itself as the individual is steadily dwarfed. All societies, capitalist or communist, are moving toward ever larger and more inclusive systems of organization, toward ever greater dominance of the system's purposes over individual purposes. There are forces at work in any such society that gravely impair the individual's ability or willingness to act on his own.

Critics often appear to believe that the smothering of individuality is a result of conscious decisions by people at the top. Right-wingers blame government leaders, left-wingers blame corporate leaders. But the modern leader is always in some measure caught in the system. To a considerable degree, the system determines how

66

and when he will exercise power. And if present trends continue, this will become more rather than less so. The queen bee is as much a prisoner of the system as is any other in the hive.

Our tradition tells us that we should be individuals, initiators, and creators, free and responsible. It tells us that every person is important. But the trend I have described transforms individuals into specialist-links in larger systems, locked into their roles, increasingly incapable of autonomous functioning.

The conflict between that harsh reality and our tradition of individual freedom and responsibility is severe and growing worse. And it could produce reactions far more acute than any we have seen to date. Men and women taught to cherish a set of values and then trapped in a system that negates those values may react with anger, even violence. Since most people are neither philosophers nor social analysts, they may be unable to say what makes them so angry. But their rage could burst to the surface, nevertheless, in spasms of disorder or wild swings of voting behavior.

Is there any way for a large, highly organized modern society, whatever its ideology, to avoid the beehive model? The honest answer has to be "perhaps." There is a possible path to salvation—not easy, not uncomplicated, but identifiable. There are a great many things we can do to redesign large-scale organization so that it is a hospitable environment for the individual. And there are many things we can do to tone up our tradition of individual freedom so that it can survive in the modern world.

We shall find it necessary to work simultaneously along two parallel lines: we must ask the individual to accept certain kinds of responsibility, and we must create the institutional framework in which individual responsibility is feasible. For example, we must ask people to participate in their community, and we must design the community so that such participation is possible. Traditionally, we have spent enormous energy exhorting the individual to act responsibly and very little energy designing the kind of society in which he *can* act responsibly. There's no possibility of being responsible if one has no community, isn't needed, and has no way of being heard.

COMMUNITY

The loss of a sense of community is particularly serious. In some ways modern society binds the individual too tightly but in other ways it holds him too loosely, and the latter causes as much pain as the former.

A man feels constrained by the conformity required in a highly organized society, but he also feels lost and without moorings. And both feelings may be traced to the same cause: the disappearance of the natural human community and its replacement by formula controls that irk, yet give no sense of security.

The significant question is not whether the individual should be completely free of his society or completely subjugated. It is a question of what are the ties and what are the freedoms. The ties must be the life-giving ties of shared values, a sense of community, a concern for the total enterprise, a sense of identity and belonging, and the opportunity to serve. The freedoms must be freedom to dissent, to be an individual, to grow and fulfill oneself, to choose in some measure one's own style and manner of serving the community.

A successful outcome of the search for meaning, purpose and identity is essential to mental health. Secure membership in a community can contribute to such an outcome. A community, however defined, is something one "belongs to," something central to one's identity, a repository of shared values and shared goals. It is an arena in which a man can see his leaders face to face and judge them as men and women, where he can know his neighbor as a whole person, not in the fragments characteristic of modern interaction.

The individual without a community—rootless, anonymous—is all too often driven to search desperately for meaning and identity. If he is young that may mean grasping at the straws of meaning offered by far-out movements. If he is older it may mean voting irrationally and unpredictably or not voting at all.

If we are to re-create a sense of community we are going to have to rediscover the means by which that sense is nurtured. And some of those means will seem "corny" to intellectuals. The modern intellectual tends to be somewhat skeptical, not always consciously, about the idea of community. And his skepticism is understandable.

Was he not justified in rejecting the restrictive forces of the old American community? Yes.

Is he not right in believing that the symbols of community (such as the flag) have often been exploited by cynical people? Yes.

Is he not right in saying that those who broke away from the old American communities created new kinds of artistic and professional excellence? Yes.

Right on every count. But now, with most of the old communities gone and nothing to take their place, we find ourselves without sources of strength and security that most human beings need very much indeed.

70

We must not be sentimental or nostalgic about communities as they once existed. We can't go home again. The old-fashioned community had a continuity, stability, and "boundedness" that simply cannot be duplicated today. (Even if it could, it's doubtful that the modern, highly mobile individual would want it that way.) Essentially, modern communities will be bases from which members can sally forth into the world. As a rule they will not have the physical separation of old-fashioned communities; more likely they will be neighborhoods in larger patterns of settlement.

We must experiment with the re-creation of communities. There are some imaginative efforts being made to create livable communities within the large university, and there are important experiments afoot to re-create a sense of community in the urban neighborhood. But we must also think in terms of new kinds of communities, some of them nongeographical. The Peace Corps at the peak of its effectiveness was, in some important respects, a community. Some of the scholarly guilds are unassembled communities. (That's one of the reasons many academic people are comfortably unaware of the loss of community throughout the rest of society.)

A good many people have noted that a sense of community can be created very swiftly by an emergency—a power blackout, a riot, a war. But that doesn't help much. The point is to get the effect without paying the price of disaster.

PARTICIPATION

Closely linked to the idea of community is the possibility of participation. Contrary to fashionable views of the moment, I do not believe that the urge to participate in the shaping of one's social institutions is a powerful human motive. It appears to me to be a notably weak and undependable impulse. But we must fan that uncertain flame.

Why? First of all, this is a moment when men and women, here and around the world, have in some measure withdrawn faith in their institutions. They are questioning, re-examining. At such a time there can be nothing more healing than for them to participate directly in the reshaping of the institutions that no longer enjoy their confidence.

Second, participation preserves the vitality of institutions and nurtures a healthy relationship between the individual and society. When people, for whatever reason —oppression, laziness, or complacency—take no part in their institutions, the institutions themselves decay at an

72

accelerating rate.

So much utter nonsense has been spoken on the subject of participation that some sensible people are allergic to the word. But the concept is as old as democracy. The question is how to give the individual a deeply rooted experience of democratic life and action in a vast and highly organized society.

It is not essential that everyone participate. As a matter of fact, if everyone suddenly did the society would fly apart. But the fact that opportunities exist and that a good many people are taking advantage of them will affect the attitude of those who don't participate. The essence of it is that participation should be an available option.

When advocates of participatory democracy urge a kind of continuous town-meeting approach to public-policy formulation they are not, of course, advocating something that would result in universal participation. It is a formula for government by those whose appetite for public meetings is insatiable.

One of the problems that must be faced honestly is how to foster participation without contributing further to the erosion of authority. Those who derive their authority from the institutions of a free society (for example, professors, college presidents, mayors) have seen their position seriously undermined in recent years. And they show it. Increasingly they act as though they doubt their own legitimacy. But a breakdown of authority moves inevitably toward the "freedom" of the alley brawl, not toward the confident self-discipline of a free people engaged in the serious business of self-government. A free people, having thrown off the tyranny of raw power, must create and honor its own structure of authority. If it ceases to do so then it moves back toward the only alternative—government by force.

The possibility of participation is closely linked to the revival of local government and local leadership. It is hard to feel individually responsible with respect to the invisible processes of a huge and distant federal government. Responsibility comes most readily when one can see the consequences of one's actions.

And that brings us to a decisive question: can action on the part of the individual at the grass roots ever really be effective? Are we calling him to a quaint and archaic task? It all depends on how we design our society. We must design it so that grass roots opinion *can* be effective. We must create the instrumentalities for citizen action.

THE QUALITY OF LIFE

All large-scale organization tends to smother individuality. This is a fact that today's young people understand better than their elders. The liberal critic of thirty years ago, if he had any doubts at all about trends in large-scale organization, would have focused his concern on the big corporation. The young person today understands that the aspects of organization that impinge on the individual are just as real in a large university, a municipal bureaucracy, a large hospital, or the federal government.

With our present massive concentrations of population there is no possibility that we can turn our backs on large-scale organization. And if we could, we wouldn't. Everyone speaks slightingly of modern technological society but no one gives up his refrigerator. Everyone condemns bigness but there is no movement of population toward the unspoiled, lonely places of the continent.

Although we cannot escape the organized aspects of modern life, we can design patterns of organization that increase our choices, enrich our lives, and do not exact an exorbitant price in surrendered individuality. Modern students of organization are beginning to identify those features of organization that strengthen the individual and those that diminish him. Given such analysis, we can begin to design institutions responsive to human need, institutions that will strengthen and nourish each person.

We have already discussed some of the ways in which that can be done—devising opportunities for participation, reviving the sense of community, providing opportunities to be heard, and releasing individual potentialities. But it isn't just large-scale organization that plagues the individual. When people say they are concerned about the "quality of life" today, they are touching on all the apprehensions of modern man, from the destruction of natural beauty to the menace of Big Brotherism. The apprehensions are real and widely shared.

It is not irresponsible to envisage a future free of such apprehensions. We do not need to be victimized by the technology that should serve us. We need not defile the countryside. We can halt the invasion of privacy. We do not need to tolerate patterns of social organization that systematically exclude our older citizens.

We can build a society to man's measure—if we have the will.

The struggle begins with the preservation of the natural resources and natural beauty of the land, and with control of environmental pollution. It extends to population control, to the use of leisure, to the pace and space of life.

OPPORTUNITY TO SERVE

One of the least recognized of human motives is the need to be needed. It is not always easily satisfied in an impersonal and fragmented society. Oddly enough, it's easier to ask for help than to ask to be needed.

A society built to man's measure will not just be one that serves him but one that gives him the opportunity to serve. It will not just be a society that does things for him but that gives him the opportunity to do something for himself and others. It will permit him the fulfillment that comes with the exercise of his talents. A justified pride in accomplishment, a feeling of having earned one's own niche is powerful medicine for the human psyche.

The experience of recent years suggests that the service idea, as exemplified in the Peace Corps and VISTA, taps a rich vein of motivation in the American people. When people are serving, life is no longer meaningless. They no longer feel rootless. They no longer feel unconnected. They feel responsible.

As we enable the individual to enjoy greater freedom, we must at the same time provide him with opportunities for allegiance and commitment to goals larger than himself. Otherwise, freedom degenerates into sterile self-preoccupation. The most troublesome consequence of self-preoccupation is boredom, and the cure for boredom is not diversion: it is to find some work to do, something to care about.

77

REPAIR OF FRAGMENTATION

Another task essential to social renewal is repair of the fragmentation produced by modern life. Our industrial civilization cuts us off from nature, and in doing so severs roots that are essential to our well-being. We are imprisoned by the abstractness and artificiality of modern life. We rarely exert ourselves; we diverge from normal cycles of waking and sleeping; our appetites and senses are schooled away from natural patterns; we fail to respect the integrity of our organisms. And we pay a price.

There are other ways in which modern life accomplishes an unhealthy fragmentation. It cuts us off from the past. It produces an artificial split between thought and emotion, between techniques and meaning. And it totally fragments the natural community.

Particularly crucial is the split between the rational, technical, planful side of life and the world of the senses, emotion, and fantasy. Have we not learned that we ignore the latter at our peril? Have we not learned that man is not just a planning, quantifying, word-and-number-manipulating animal, but a creature of dreams and impulse and appetite, hungry for sensory experience, needful of emotional release? It is a side of our nature that will not allow itself to be excluded. If it has no accepted place in a cultural framework that sets moral and legal boundaries, it will create its own secret world and burst to the surface in unpredictable outbreaks.

The fragmentation is not simply between intellect and emotion. We all seek in one way or another a return to the wholeness of an earlier day when man was not cut off from nature or from his fellow man. When, through some transforming experience (a great love, a great emergency, a great religious experience), a measure of unity is re-established, we learn how powerful is the impulse to absorption of the self in a larger whole, how intoxicating are the emotions released—so intoxicating that people seek the experience through drugs, through chiliastic movements, through the exhilaration of mob action.

But all of the fragmentation is not caused by impersonal trends in the organization of modern society. Some of it is caused by modern man himself, who seems at times to be seized with a frenzied impulse to shatter every last vestige of continuity and coherence in the forms and patterns of social living.

SELF-DISCIPLINE

In the same way that modern man obsessively breaks up the patterns of life and then finds himself nervous and afraid in a formless world, so—in the name of freedom—he compulsively dissolves the limits on behavior and then finds himself frightened in a world without limits. He sweeps aside rules, manners, formalities, and standards of taste—anything that inhibits the free play of emotion and impulse. But in a world of imperfect people, some of them savage, some undisciplined, some foolish, some rapacious, civilization is built on restraints. Some of the restraints are written into law, but in a free society a great many are internalized in the breast of the free citizen. They are unwritten, voluntary, a matter of custom and convention.

Every step toward removal of arbitrary constraints on individual behavior must be accompanied by increments in self-imposed controls. Self-discipline is the free man's yoke. Either he is his own master or he will be his own slave—not merely a slave to his passions, as an earlier generation might have feared, but a slave to his unbounded ego. All who have observed the distinctive pathologies of modern life must be impressed by the expansive capacities of the ego. Nurtured on dreams of man's perfectibility, it is only briefly satisfied with the freedom gained from the decline of religion, custom and authority. It must go on to reject all that may limit it—all rules, requirements, and traditional roles. History is shrugged off because to absorb it requires discipline.

Reason is rejected because it imposes irksome constraints. The imperious self measures all restraints in terms of its own need for ascendancy.

Not only the claims of civility but the realities of individual development call for some measure of self-discipline. Every great artistic performance is the consequence of self-discipline long and faithfully applied. So is every great athletic or intellectual performance. Discipline in that sense—schooling, a conscious adherence to standards, an effort to bring performance into line with an admired ideal—is the essence of craftsmanship.

Apprenticeship is rejected by some today as a distasteful subordination. But they reject along with it (whether they know it or not) the whole tradition of craftsmanship, mastery, diligence in learning, and excellence in performance. You can't vote yourself into the company of great heart surgeons and concert pianists.

Aversion to the necessary inequalities of the teacher-student relationship is expressed by some college students today. What they fail to understand is that any society, even a primitive one, is a complex pattern of interlocking roles. To wash out the differentiation of roles makes the total performance impossible. The male dancer who catches the ballerina must not demand that she in turn catch him. Professors should seek to understand the

81

needs of their students but should not forsake their role or doubt its legitimacy. With respect to the subject they are teaching, there is an inequality that can only be erased through the process of learning.

CHAPTER FIVE

Leadership and Common Purpose

Each nation has the government it deserves.

—DeMaistre

ONE HEARS it asserted by intelligent men that the swift pace of change and the complexity of interacting forces have rendered our society—and the world—essentially unmanageable. These are men who have thought long and hard about perils the rest of us don't like to contemplate—the rate of population increase throughout the world, the rate at which we are polluting the thin atmospheric envelope of our planet, the terrifying possibilities of nuclear or biological warfare, the future of the cities.

I do not share the view that our situation is irretrievable, but we had better be honest with ourselves about our capacity to cope with our troubles.

The complexity of the social forces affecting us is beyond our present powers of analysis and measurement. Except for the fairly well developed field of economics, we are just taking the first fumbling steps in the development of "social indicators" to measure various dimensions of social functioning. Until we progress further in our modes of analysis, we shall be repeatedly surprised by the consequences of social forces we can neither comprehend nor describe.

The pace of change is even more central to our difficulty. Problems evolve with frightening speed. By the time the alarm bell sounds it is almost too late for corrective action. All of which puts a premium on our ability to see ahead. We're like a man driving eighty miles per hour in a fog that permits him to see only thirty feet ahead. In a horse and buggy thirty feet would have been adequate. Everyone is a little bored with those probers of the future who speculate solemnly about the year 2000, but in fact they are responding adaptively.

It has not escaped notice, of course, that some of our most perplexing problems are ones we created for ourselves. Chief among them are the troubles that stem from our Faustian zest in plunging after every technological possibility that promises profit or power or pleasure. We act at once and live with the consequences. The list is long and growing longer—food additives, radiation poisoning, environmental contaminants, and so on. What lies ahead in the realm of biological meddling is hair-raising in its possibilities.

Not all of our problem lies in failures of social analysis and social forecasting. After we see what we must do, there is the matter of summoning our forces to act. And in that we exhibit the gravest deficiencies.

The crises that concern us most deeply are not, typically, matters that can be solved by people acting individually. The crises require public management in behalf of the total community. And at that level we are woefully weak.

THE BINDING ELEMENT IN PLURALISM

We pride ourselves on having a system in which power and initiative are widely distributed. There is a great variety of institutions, none of which is locked into a single, all-embracing hierarchy. We like it that way.

It is a particularly beneficent environment for the flowering of special parts of the society—the business world, the universities, the unions, the professions—each of which can pursue its own course of development without the constricting bonds of a rigid, all-inclusive system.

But pluralism has a weakness, and we had better think hard about that weakness if we are to preserve the system. The danger is that the many independent elements in the system find it almost impossible to work together in achieving any common purpose. And a system that cannot pursue its common purposes effectively will not long survive. It will sooner or later lose all coherence, all sense of direction, all capacity to achieve the shared goals of its members.

Pluralism in this society today is built on a functional division of labor. And deep in our tradition is the notion that if everyone pursues his own business the common interest will be served.

The only trouble is that it isn't true. Observe the cities today. Each group—business, labor, the universities, the professions, the schools, the hospitals—does its specialized work but neither individually nor collectively are they doing the things that will solve the city's problems. Indeed, some of those problems arose precisely because no one of the special interests, nor all of them together, was paying much attention.

Unfortunately, the role of the special interests goes considerably beyond not "paying much attention." Each person and each group guards with fanatic zeal the tent peg that holds his corner of the system in place—and taken all together, the innumerable vested interests frustrate and subvert plans for the common good.

In short, pluralism needs some binding principle, some instrumentality for insuring that common purposes are in fact accomplished.

The obvious instrumentality for dealing with issues that cut across special fields is government. But government, particularly at the local level, has too often become just another element in the pluralism, no more inclined than any of the other elements to concern itself with overarching problems. In the case of local government, one can explain the failure by noting that it has been starved and neglected by the electorate. It is harder to explain the failure of the federal government. Only those who know the federal government very well indeed know how disinclined it is to think in the largest terms about the nation's future.

Government at every level, properly conceived and organized, can lend coherence to our efforts without smothering the private sector. But that will only happen if we undertake a far-reaching overhaul of our governmental machinery. Failing that, we shall continue to see our pluralism drift helplessly toward chaos.

We are approaching that condition in this society

today. Individual purposes are well served. Probably in no society in the world have so many persons had both the freedom and affluence to satisfy individual whims. But our common purposes—education, law enforcement and the administration of justice, a livable environment, and so on—are for the most part seriously neglected.

GOVERNMENT

We need not enlarge an already unwieldy government apparatus, but we must make it vastly more effective for specified purposes. We have not managed by our neglect of the machinery of government to make that machinery less obtrusive. Lacking any countervailing force of knowing criticism by citizens, it has proliferated at every level. It is huge. It is expensive. It is ubiquitous. And still it does not serve our purposes. Every day at every level, outworn governmental machinery is wasting taxpayers' money, thwarting the efforts of elected leaders, and frustrating the citizenry.

The issue is central to the urban crisis. It is astonishing that local government performs as well as it does, given the handicaps under which it labors. Most cities are monstrosities from a governmental point of view. The typical metropolitan area is fragmented nonsensically into dozens, even hundreds, of political jurisdictions. City officials are typically underpaid. The mayor or city manager rarely has either the authority or money or personnel to do an adequate job of governing. The machinery of city government is usually antiquated. City ordinances are riddled with provisions designed to favor or protect vested interests.

And the root of all those problems is public apathy. If the American people want local government that is more efficient and honest and responsive, they can have it.

But the redesign of city government isn't enough. We must greatly strengthen the capacity of the states to play an informed, constructive role in urban affairs; we need far better articulation of federal, state, and local efforts; and we need greatly improved federal organization for dealing with domestic problems.

Both anger and sentimentality have clouded the debate over federal versus grass-roots initiative. For thirty-five years the dominant political thinking in the nation asserted that the answer to every problem was more federal legislation, more federal dollars, bigger federal programs. Conservatives disagreed, but they never lifted a finger to strengthen state and local government. Then in the 1960's, with an enormous new burst of federally initiated activity, everyone learned some hard lessons.

We learned how failures of coordination at the federal

level lead to fatal confusion at the local level. We learned how crucial is effective team play between higher and lower levels of government. And we learned over and over how local failures could nullify the most carefully drafted federal legislation.

Students of the political process have long been skeptical of the potentialities of local government. They know how mediocre it has been. They doubt that it will ever attract top talent. They know that the American people do not offer their nearest officials much opportunity to be statesmanlike. And they know that nothing is entirely local any more.

But they are in the process of discovering that centralized government also has its weaknesses, that too much centralization falls of its own weight, that the federal government cannot (and as a matter of sound procedure should not) solve complex local problems. They are beginning to see that the federal government can insure its effectiveness *only* by making more flexible delegations of power to state and local government and to the private sector.

The debate over centralization versus decentralization will never be settled, and in fact does not pose the relevant choice. This huge and complex society cannot function without a strong federal government. Nor can it function without vital and effective state and local levels.

90

What is important is that the functions of governing be as-
signed wisely among the various levels of government so
that we can pursue vigorously those problems that require a national solution while at the same time strengthening state and local governments to do what only they
can do.

For anyone with an interest in how men govern themselves, the improvement of our governmental machinery
to meet the issues of today poses problems that are in-
comparably puzzling and challenging. It involves constitutional questions rivaling those that faced the founders
of this nation. It seems likely that the restructuring so essential at state and local levels will not occur without the
leverage of federal funds granted under conditions that
provide the incentive for change.

PUBLIC AND PRIVATE SECTORS

For a generation we have listened to debates
which assume that conflict between the public and private sectors could (and perhaps should) end in a lopsided
victory for one or the other. Now we know that the best
thing for continuance of our system is an interplay that
strengthens both.

In any community a high proportion of the executive

talent, analytical skill, and institutional strength lies outside city government. Unless means are found to mobilize those private-sector strengths in behalf of public purposes, the community will not solve its problems.

At the national level, there is a long history of public-private collaboration (tax exemption for educational institutions, subsidies and tax credits for farmers and businessmen, research support for universities, and so on). Legislation of recent years carries that collaboration much further.

But the success of the collaboration depends on the detailed design of the relationship. The government can design its relationships with the universities, for example, in such a way as to diminish their freedom—or it can strengthen and preserve their freedom. Which consequence ensues depends on how the legislation is drafted, how departmental regulations are written, the conditions imposed, the accounting practices followed, and so on.

The same is true of government relations with business. There are many forms of federal involvement with business—contracts, subsidies, tax credits, and the like. Each has its consequences for the character of the relationship. Over the years we have constructed an enormous variety of such relations, but we have been so caught up in the rhetoric of the business-versus-government debate that we still have no adequate analytical

grasp of the consequences of one or another kind of involvement.

LEADERSHIP

An important thing to understand about any
institution or social system is that it doesn't move unless it's pushed. And what is generally needed is not a mild
push but a solid jolt. If the push is not administered by
vigorous and purposeful leaders, it will be administered
eventually by an aroused citizenry or by a crisis. Sys-
temic inertia is characteristic of every human institution, but overwhelmingly true of this nation as a whole.
Our system of checks and balances dilutes the thrust of
positive action. The competition of interests inherent in
our pluralism acts as a brake on concerted action. The
system grinds to a halt between crises. Madison designed
it in such a way that it simply won't move without vigorous leadership. I've often wondered why he didn't say so.
Perhaps, having in mind his brilliant contemporaries, it
just never occurred to him that the day might come
when leadership would be lacking.

We have moderately effective leadership in the specialized worlds that make up our society, but we need something more. We need leaders who can move beyond their

93

special fields to deal with problems of the total community. That we have too few is hardly surprising. The modern world is in love with specialization. Most of our ablest young people specialize. And then when we find that broad-gauged leaders are in short supply, all the specialists say, "What have we done to deserve such poor leadership?"

Despite the pressures of specialization, the young person with leadership gifts might find time to develop those gifts—if he were encouraged. He is not encouraged. Many of his professors convey the impression that the important issues are solved by men who develop their professional skills, analyze problems, and apply formulas. Rarely does anyone tell him that many (perhaps most) of the great issues are settled in the push and pull of the public forum, in an atmosphere of confusion that is alien to good professional standards but inseparable from the process of orchestrating human purposes and resolving conflicts.

Analysts and experts are needed, even in dealing with intensely political issues—needed, for example, to help determine priorities. But leaders are needed too, particularly at the national level. They may turn to experts for help. They themselves may have been experts at an earlier stage. But as leaders they must have skills that go beyond specialized education. They must deal with those inherently untidy situations in which two equally worthy constituents (or groups) want mutually exclusive things. They must assert a vision of the nation as it might be, and summon us to the sacrifice needed to achieve it. They must keep hope alive, hope that despite the gravity of our problems, despite our own frailties and occasional savagery, we can gain command of our situation and ourselves.

DIFFICULTIES OF LEADERSHIP TODAY

The schools and colleges not only persuade the young person that most of the world's problems are solved by experts, they teach him in subtle ways (perhaps without fully intending it) to be somewhat contemptuous of leaders.

He gains the clear impression from his teachers that the professional man is pure in his motivation and high in his standards; does not become involved in controversy; does not demean himself by becoming entangled in the push and pull of power conflict. In contrast, he gains the impression from his mentors that leaders (politicians, college presidents, corporate executives) are corrupt. They compromise. They make deals. They are ambitious. They lack integrity. They are morally less worthy than those who toil in the antiseptic environment of the laboratory and the study. The message, intended or not, comes through clearly: don't be a leader; be a professional.

Yet anyone who knows university faculties, scientific laboratories, and the professions knows that they too are the scene of compromise, vested interest, jealousy, rivalry, power conflict, and all the other corrupting forces. But unlike corruption in public life, the quiet compromise of integrity in the laboratory, studio, or professional suite rarely comes to public attention. It is almost inaudible.

It is true that power often corrupts; so, too, do vanity, complacency, timidity, moral arrogance, and a hunger for security, none of which is unknown in the laboratory and the study.

Someone must perform the tasks of leadership. If our most gifted and idealistic young people are driven away, less able and idealistic people will fill the vacuum. If we scorn the tasks of leadership then we must not complain when public life is taken over by buffoons and counterfeiters.

I am not suggesting that every young person be trained as a leader. Many would neither enjoy nor be fitted for it. But the small proportion of young people who show a natural capacity for leadership should be gratefully encouraged and provided with opportunities to develop the gift.

Leadership involves special difficulties today. For one thing, all but the highest-ranking leaders must operate from a position of virtual anonymity. There was a time when communities were small enough and life was simple enough so that even minor and local leaders enjoyed a prominence that is out of the question today. The high decibel level in our society makes it immensely difficult for leaders to gain attention for worthwhile objectives.

Add to that the complexity of the issues. Untutored good judgment, the chief asset of leaders since the dawn of history, is no longer enough. The leader must have some command, however rudimentary, of the social and technical issues that will affect his choices.

But there is a more serious circumstance complicating the task of the leader today. For whatever reasons, this is a time when people—here and around the world—are withdrawing the confidence they have reposed in their institutions, and this poses almost insuperable difficulties for the leader. People with confidence in their institutions are willing to delegate decisions to their leaders (congressmen, cardinals, governors, union officials). When confidence wanes, they withdraw the delegation.

Derision and contempt are common fare for leaders these days. There exists among many segments of the populace a sour mixture of apathy and negativism. The average citizen, feeling vaguely coerced by an impersonal society, trained in the passivity of the spectator, experiencing no sense of personal responsibility, looks at the leader with a mean and ungracious skepticism. What can he do for me? Why should I trust him?

REFLECTION AND ACTION

The role of the leader is complicated by the serious (and perhaps growing) chasm between the worlds of reflection and action. Each of those worlds must preserve its own integrity. But they need not be—must not be—wholly out of touch.

I have discussed the problem at length in earlier writings;* let me illustrate just one aspect of the difficulty here. The most profound and eloquent contemporary diagnoses of the human condition are being produced by artists, writers, philosophers, dramatists, and scholars who are professionally separated from the world of action and decision. They tend to write for (and expect to be judged by) others who are equally separated from the decisive action of the world.

* Particularly in *No Easy Victories* (New York: Harper & Row, 1968).

98

The world of action has its own "literature", and some of it is of excellent quality but for the most part it steers clear of (or deals shallowly with) the moral and philosophical questions that agitate the minds of all modern men, whether they act or observe. If men and women in the world of action want to explore those questions in depth they must turn, as a rule, to the learned and literary world. And there they find themselves in the hands of people who have cut themselves off from the dilemmas of action.

As contrasted with the world of reflection and analysis, the world of action is characterized by the coercive character of the decisions facing the individual. One is forced to choose; not to choose becomes a form of choice. One faces multiple decisions at the same time, some of which interrelate in complex ways. Making the "right" decision on one issue endangers a favorable outcome on a second issue. Decisions must be made on available evidence, however scanty. And one must not only act, but act with vigor and confidence. Those who live in the world of action are held to a form of testing that is imprecise but relentless: both their values and their hypotheses are tested in the doing.

When the intellectual world cuts all of its ties with the world of performance it loses the capacity to appraise action or to recommend courses of action. Most of the totally despairing social diagnoses ("the System can't be made to work") come from individuals so separated from the workings of the System that if it *could* be made to work they would be the last to know.

The best social criticism comes from individuals who have in one way or another brought about some distance between themselves and the institution criticized. But when the separation becomes too great, when the critic keeps himself so carefully separated from the world of action that he can't understand the assumptions, constraints and realities of the system, then the criticism loses validity.

Many of our critics suffer from just such excessive separation. And many idealistic young people today actively seek such separation. Insulation from the corrupting world is attractive to them. They are hostile to the central institutions of the society and welcome the opportunity to stay "outside."

It is essential to combat the growing notion that the farther you are from the action the purer you are. When young people, in the service of that notion, seek to hold themselves clear of society's central institutions, they are entertaining an unworthy purpose.

It is too easy to sit outside the arena of action and lob mortar shells of criticism into the center. Milton said, "I cannot praise a fugitive and cloistered virtue . . . that never sallies out and seeks her adversary, but slinks out of the race where that immortal garland is to be run for, not without dust and heat."

Some good men must indeed stay outside the circle of action, as scholars, artists, critics, philosophers. But other good men belong in the heat of the battle, where the issues are confused, where you're never sure you're right, where good and bad are inextricably fused with the partly good and partly bad, where often you can't do one worthy thing without endangering some other worthy thing.

And some, at least, of the world's philosophers, scholars, writers, and artists should understand the imperatives of action and the qualities essential to action. This does not mean that they will be less critical of the man of action. They may, in important respects, be tougher because they will be able to aim their criticism more effectively. Criticism is needed. Men of action, precisely because of the hard necessities under which they operate, often engage in self-deceiving justifications, fail to examine their assumptions, fail to apply rigorous evaluative measures, neglect the weighing of priorities, mistake the urgent for the important, follow the path of expediency, wallow in self-congratulation, and defend the status quo. Often they need the most vigorous lambasting that critics can administer.

But they need something in addition to criticism. They need help. They need to be ministered to in ways that cannot readily occur in an adversary relationship. They need perspective; they need to see their tasks in a philosophic framework; they need to understand the depth and complexity of the cultural currents with which they deal; they need a sense of history; sometimes they need to be saved from shallow, perhaps even dangerous, "muscular" philosophies of action.

The world of learning and reflection stands equally to gain by a closer relationship. It must, for the sake of its own full comprehension of life, gain a better understanding of the complexities of action.

CHAPTER SIX

Self-Contempt and Hope

Dum spiro, spero.

I T IS GENERALLY recognized that there is a relationship between what others expect of us and what we expect of ourselves. When one group oppresses another, the most tragic consequence may be that the oppressed group accepts and believes in its own inferiority. It is an ever-present problem in the education of minority-group children. Their teachers often do not believe them to be capable of high performance, and what the teachers believe becomes a self-fulfilling prophecy. The fact that the teachers may be of the same minority group as the children doesn't eliminate the possibility of such attitudes.

EXPECTATIONS AND PERFORMANCE

The problem is not limited to race but extends to all teaching. If the teacher expects more of the learner, the learner expects more of himself—and performs better. There are exceptions and qualifications, but the principle is of ruling importance.

The principle extends far beyond the formal teaching relationship. In any field, the individual's knowledge of what others expect of him may affect both his self-image and his ability to perform. If others see him as a loser, it is harder to see himself as a winner. If he thinks he is worthless, it is harder to prove himself worthy.

The principle is exemplified by young people in difficulty with the law. Everyone who has worked with youthful offenders knows that a young person has a hard time staying out of trouble if everyone expects him to get *into* trouble. That is why enlightened methods of dealing with such a youngster postpone as long as possible the day when he must be officially labeled delinquent. And one of the puzzles of rehabilitation is how he can go back to his old neighborhood and not be affected by the widely shared view that he is a person of whom no good can be expected. It's an old story, and the effect on the young person is predictable. If he is not accepted as part of the respectable community, why bother to act respectable?

Among those who often expect the worst of the youthful offender are the police. And ironically, the police are now on the receiving end of the same expectations of antisocial behavior—with the same results. If the police are to perform in an admirable way, it is essential that they have high morale and an image of themselves that incorporates all the good things we want them to be. And how are they to have that self-image when those who would most wish them to improve vilify them indiscriminately? If they are to make themselves better people, they must first of all believe that they have it in them to be better people. To read them out of the company of civilized men does not move them toward virtue.

The principle of the self-fulfilling prophecy is powerfully at work here, because we are dealing with a group that one may join or leave at will. If we surround our police with an atmosphere of contempt, good men will not sign up and good men already in will leave, so that gradually the force will conform to the image held by its worst critics.

Now apply the principle to the whole society. A so-

105

ciety capable of greatness must be confident that it has the spiritual and other strengths to rise to great performance. It must have the confidence to criticize itself, but its self-affirming sentiments will outweigh the criticism.

If this is true, then those who wish us to behave with greatness and generosity as a nation should encourage us to believe that we are capable of exhibiting such qualities. We are about as far from that situation today as we can be. There has grown up in our midst what might be described as a self-contemptuous culture. It consists of substantial numbers of Americans who are scornful of their own society.

CRITICISM VERSUS CONTEMPT

I used the phrase "self-contemptuous culture," but almost everyone who exhibits the tendency exempts himself from the criticism. He sees *other* Americans as the appropriate target.

Let me be clear about the relation of such contempt to hard-hitting criticism. Many of the most searing critics of this society have *not* been contemptuous of it. From Lincoln Steffens to Ralph Nader, from Upton Sinclair to Michael Harrington, there is a tradition of criticism that is tough-minded but not rejecting. It calls a spade a spade, it cuts through hypocrisy, it exposes rascals, it identifies specific and concrete evils to be eliminated. But in addressing the society, it says between the lines (as all great teachers say between the lines), "You have it in you to do better."

The contemptuous tradition is something else again. Far from stimulating people to do battle against the forces of evil, it chills and depresses. It drains away courage. It lowers morale. If citizens are to go into action for liberty and truth, they need to believe that they are capable of fighting the good fight. The contemptuous tradition offers them only fear and guilt and a pervasive sense of unworthiness. And by making a generalized and vaguely defined "society" the object of its scorn, it diminishes the individual's will to do battle against specific and perhaps surmountable problems.

The contemptuous tradition has its own rhetoric and postures that infect all social criticism today. Thus when it becomes necessary to attack racism, one finds many critics framing their attack in terms so withering that the whole society lies prostrate before them. They leave no room for the belief that we have in us a grain of virtue on which to build a better future.

One encounters the contemptuous attitude everywhere —in the communications media, in the "new" films, in popular songs, in the fashion magazines, in the classroom. In the same way, the alienated posture has become commandingly fashionable. Once the more or less exclusive property of artists and intellectuals (whose alienation was usually authentic), the attitudes of alienation have long since spread to great numbers of educated Americans, and beyond them to many of the technicians of the educated class, and beyond them to hangers-on and camp followers. The language of alienation is common currency. It appears in chic articles on fashion, in cheap commercial TV shows, and in slick advertisements.

No doubt there have been alienated people in every society and in every age. What is new in history is the emergence of the alienated style as a fashionable, often profitable, role. And alienation as a modish pose clouds the diagnosis of alienation as a serious ailment.

DISSENT AND LEADERSHIP

Two critically important social processes—dissent and leadership—are complicated by the rise of "fashionable alienation."

Dissent is a serious and honorable pursuit. Those who are engaged in the grueling work of accomplishing institutional change are in desperate need of allies.

The responsible critic is of enormous help in identifying targets for action, in clarifying and focusing issues, in formulating significant goals and mobilizing support for those goals. He comes to understand the complex machinery by which change must be accomplished, finds the key points of leverage, and identifies feasible alternatives. We have many such critics, and we owe them a great debt.

The responsible critic has not rejected his culture. Disturbed by some aspect of the mainstream of his culture, he works to alter that condition so that he can admire his culture unreservedly. If he is intelligent and honest he never achieves total peace because there are always elements of injustice that he must combat. But the tension and striving are always there to eliminate the evil and again embrace one's culture.

With the enormous fashionableness of the alienated posture, however, there has emerged another kind of critic, one who has discovered that the "alienated" position is profitable, diverting, and a great ego-inflator. Once he has made that discovery, the goal of curing social evils begins, in infinitely subtle ways, to lose reality. In fact, the existence of social evils becomes an important part of his psychic economy; they are magnificent stage props for his act. He no longer seeks redemption for his society. His eye is on the audience.

109

Such a critic never exposes himself to the tough tests of reality. He doesn't limit himself to feasible options. He doesn't subject his view of the world to the cleansing discipline of historical perspective. He shrugs off the constraints that limit action in the real world.

It's a hard game to lose. If such a critic takes care to stay outside the arena of action and decision, his judgment and integrity will never be tested, never risked, never laid on the line. He can feel a limitless moral superiority to the mere mortals who put their reputation at hazard every day in accountable action. He can spin fantasies of what might be without the heart-breaking, back-breaking work of building social change into resistant human institutions.

The worst that can be said of such mountebanks is that they obscure and confuse the signals from serious critics. In the same way, the large numbers of people today who "play at alienation" obscure and confuse the dilemma of the truly alienated.

Every culture resists criticism, and no critic can be effective unless he establishes some measure of independence or separation from his culture. Today he has a dual struggle—to free himself from the pressures toward conformity in his culture and to fight free of the equally seductive pressures of fashionable dissent.

The other social function that is endangered by fash-

110

ionable scorn for the mainstream of the culture is leadership. It is reasonable to expect that a considerable share of the leadership in any society will be supplied by the ablest, most educated, and most articulate citizens. But it is precisely among such citizens that the attitudes of fashionable contempt for the culture have been most prevalent.

A good many people of superior education today exhibit a contempt for the rest of the society that reaches beyond the scope of rigorous social criticism and approximates the arrogance of all privileged classes throughout history. To put it bluntly, they scorn the things the common man respects and laugh at the things he loves.

One can understand the temptation. There is nothing more surely ego-inflating than to feel oneself part of a worldly-wise minority that sees through the general foolishness.

But if the most gifted, talented, and articulate members of society will not accept the burdens of leadership, who will? And how will they lead a people of whom they are contemptuous?

How ironic it will be if history records that the most democratic educational system in the world produced an educated class that scorned the rest of the society, outraged the sensibilities of the man in the street, and could not lead because it could not conceal its contempt for the people who might have been its followers.

Out of the ranks of educated Americans must come much of our most effective dissent and enlightened leadership. Neither role will be enhanced if they succumb to the cheap but fashionable postures of contempt for the majority of their fellow citizens. Their duty is to teach, criticize, reform, persuade, and push—but not with contempt. Their mission is not to lord it over the boobs but to stimulate, to set examples, to create models and to lead.

If we are to survive we must accomplish a far-reaching overhaul of our institutions. We need leaders. We need critics. We need citizens who are dissatisfied with things as they are and impatient to move forward. We don't need self-contempt.

THE MYTH OF REGRESS

Those whose gifts fit them for leadership must recognize that a prime function of the leader is to keep hope alive. And that is going to require a further examination of currently fashionable attitudes.

Once we accepted the Myth of Progress and were all stupidly certain that historical forces would carry us inevitably on and up. Then the myth was exploded and replaced, over time, by a Myth of Regress. In the judgment of many of our most gifted contemporaries, nothing ever gets better, it only gets worse. Orwell said of certain modern writers, "All of them are temperamentally hostile to the notion of 'progress'; it is felt that progress not only doesn't happen, but *ought not* to happen."

One hears on every hand the most gloomy diagnoses of our situation. And one source of gloom is a curious cycle we go through with respect to social problems. It may be illustrated by our concern for the disadvantaged child. Ten or fifteen years ago the phrase was hardly known. Almost no one worried about the fact that the educational system might be doing less than enough for the child of poverty. Then we discovered him. In a decade we have made him the subject of an avalanche of studies. His plight is known to every literate American. Scores, even hundreds, of new approaches to his education have been launched. For good or ill, billions of dollars are being spent on him annually that weren't being spent before. And how do we feel after a decade of commendable action in behalf of the disadvantaged child? Miserable! We are now keenly aware of a problem that we had blissfully ignored and feel acutely depressed that we are not doing as much as we should.

Forty years ago we were, by today's standards, shockingly ignorant of the problems of race discrimination.

Even twenty years ago we were incredibly neglectful of race problems. Now, after two decades of unprecedented attention and unprecedented gains, are we happy and proud that we have faced up to the problem and are trying to solve it? Not at all. With our new awareness, we see the issue in its true dimensions and are desperately impatient to do more—so impatient that we brush off past gains as trivial.

Impatience is essential. But when it leads us to deny that any progress at all has been made, it deprives us of the confidence to face the hard battles ahead. Past successes are what give people the courage to go on.

It isn't enough for leaders to sketch a vision of the future. They must prepare people for the frustrations of getting there, and they must persuade them that they have it in them to get there.

SELF-PITY AND SELF-EXONERATION

To accomplish the hard tasks of social change requires exceptional stamina, particularly among those who must take the lead. The individual is more likely to exhibit the necessary fortitude if he has immunized himself against two raging and pestilential modern disorders: self-pity and self-exoneration.

114

Today we are greatly impressed with the impact of environment on the individual. We know the powerful effect an unfavorable environment can have. We want to surround every child with the conditions that will be favorable to growth, to learning, to the flowering of whatever talent he may have.

So far so good. But the environmental explanation is so popular today that every felon can discourse on the evil conditions that made him what he is. He may be correct. But there is a menacing danger to the individual who accepts such a theory. It relieves him of responsibility. It saps his will to command the part of his fate that is his to command. It opens the door to self-pity. And self-pity is easily the most destructive of the nonpharmaceutical narcotics. It is addictive, gives momentary pleasure, and separates the victim from reality.

It is proper—indeed essential—for society to call attention to the ill effects of an unfavorable environment. But the strategy for any individual who wants to remain whole and strong must be radically different. Far from dwelling on the consequences of environment, he must remind himself of the many cases in which individuals rise above their environment. If he is to avoid becoming a moral cripple he must refuse to divest himself of moral responsibility for his acts.

Today a great many affluent and educated people are

115

blaming their own misbehavior on the irrationality or corruption or "absurdity" of society, which is another way of saying that they are no longer personally responsible but that society is responsible. It is a particularly neat trick because the most advanced practitioners of the art think of themselves as individualists. And, of course, in half their lives they are. They favor individualism in impulse, but communal responsibility ("I do what I please; but if what I do is bad, blame the society").

But a people who hand moral responsibility over to the society will eventually have their impulses brought under control by society.

HOPE

In the world of action, hope is of the essence. But hope is out of style. It is taken by some to be a mark of the sheerest vulgarity. Unrelieved pessimism is the fashionable mood. All good omens are promptly discounted as part of the plastic hypocrisy of modern life.

We have all reacted against naïve optimism, the optimism that believes everything will come out all right, that imagines it has found a sure path to salvation.

I speak for another kind of optimism, an optimism that does not assume it has found a cure for all of life's

ills, that recognizes the deep, intrinsic difficulties in social change, that accepts life's often unfavorable odds—
but will not stop hoping, or trying, or enjoying when it's
possible to enjoy.

No doubt the world is, among other things, a vale of
tears. It is full of absurdities that cannot be explained,
evils that cannot be countenanced, injustices that cannot
be excused. The individual who does not understand that
is disarmed in a hazardous environment.

But then there is the resilience of the human spirit.
Hope runs deeper than intellectual appraisal. We were designed for struggle, for survival. Only fatal and final inju-
ries neutralize that irrepressible striving toward the light.
Our conscious processes—the part of us that is saturated
with words and ideas—may arrive at exceedingly
gloomy appraisals, but an older, more deeply rooted, bi-
ologically and spiritually stubborn part of us continues
to say yes to hoping, yes to striving, yes to life.

In short, there are many whose impulse to constructive action is too deeply rooted to be touched by the current fashion of despair. They may know how difficult it
is to better the lot of men; they may know all the ambig-
uities of rational social action; they may know that we
shall never escape the tragedy of the human condition.
But they intend to do what they can.

If there is a long chance that we can replace brutality

with reason, inequity with justice, ignorance with enlightenment, we must try. And our chances are better if we have not convinced ourselves that the cause is hopeless. All effective action is fueled by hope. Pessimism may be an acceptable attitude in literary and artistic circles, but in the world of action it is the soil in which desperate and extreme solutions germinate, among them reaction and brutal oppression.

It is not given to man to know the worth of his efforts. It is arrogant of the individual to imagine that he has grasped the larger design of life and discovered that effort is worthless, especially if that effort is calculated to accomplish some immediate increment in the dignity of a fellow human. Who is he to say it is useless? His business as a man is to try.

CHAPTER SEVEN

The Renewal of Values

*Man is the only animal that laughs and weeps;
for he is the only animal that is struck with the
difference between what things are, and what they
ought to be.*

—*Hazlitt*

WE CAN MAKE great progress in improving the functioning of our society and still not have
anything that will live or last unless we concern ourselves
with the values that underlie the enterprise.

The individual today is exposed to many radically differing value systems. In the past—in a world not yet
transformed by communication and transportation—the

individual lived as a rule in a community that shared a sense of what was permissible. He saw a good deal of unseemly behavior, but it fell into predictable categories—adultery, cruelty, greed—and was carried on in fairly conventional ways. Today on television, in the newspapers and magazines, in novels and plays, in popular books on sex and anthropology he is exposed to virtually every value system ever held by any human being. And given our contemporary preoccupation with the pathological, much that he sees has to do with deviations from the main trends of human behavior, with feverish and distorted values, with the casualties and monstrosities of life.

THE INTERNAL GYROSCOPE

Can a society survive if its members are being constantly bombarded with information and images reflecting radically variant value systems? Do humans need to be allowed to live in a more orderly environment of values? Or do we need to develop a new cultural type, an individual able to live in a chaotic environment because he has developed the gift of creating his own order, because he has a powerful internal gyroscope? As I see it, that is the only possible solution.

120

But we are not very good at producing that kind of individual. We are skilled in producing skeptics, but not very good at producing individuals who can create their own framework of values.

The modern intellectual is no friend of received beliefs and traditional assumptions. He favors skepticism. He turns every familiar idea upside down and shakes it. The high school teacher and college professor pride themselves on jarring young people out of the conventional beliefs with which their minds are furnished.

But it has become increasingly clear that large numbers of people never find anything to replace those shattered early beliefs. And it is increasingly apparent that people who have nothing they can believe in are subject to a whole compendium of strange ailments. Neither pleasure nor profit nor freedom nor busyness fills the void.

Not all are equally vulnerable. Some appear either to thrive on skepticism or perhaps to draw on springs of unconscious belief. But others want and need some core of conscious conviction around which to organize their lives. The depth of that need is seen in the fact that many people forsake traditional beliefs only to fall head over heels into some half-baked political or social dogma of the moment. The need to believe is there, and if denied one vessel, seeks others. One would suppose that the individual who had fought his way out of the web of traditional beliefs would approach new commitments with caution and intellectual discipline. Some do. But others embrace new beliefs with an intemperate and undiscriminating ardor, thirstily, "as the hart panteth after the waterbrooks."

Teachers are right to demand that young people re-examine the received beliefs of childhood. That is a part of growing up as a thinking person. But after the shakeup, the individual must reconstruct a framework of values that is right for him and relevant to his time. And available evidence indicates that most individuals are not well equipped for the search. Can we help them?

It is possible. We have never really tried. Those stimulating instructors who shatter the student's conventional beliefs don't tell him how to pick up the pieces and move on to values that will serve him well.

As we set out to explore the question, we would do well to dispose of one issue immediately: must a new framework of values be scientifically proven? The old value systems began to disintegrate as science emerged, and it is widely believed that the two events were linked, that science killed the old belief systems. But that is not entirely true. Science dissolved some of the fabric of superstition and myth clinging to old beliefs, but the breakdown of beliefs was a part of the disintegration of *all* premodern cultural systems, not only religions but political philosophies, social dogmas, customs and folkways. Among the solvents other than science were revolutionary advances in transportation and communication, and the impact of the Industrial Revolution on all the structures of society.

But the question remains as to whether any new framework of values can emerge unless it is sanctioned by science. The first thing to be said is that there is little future for a framework of values which asserts as true things that science knows to be untrue. Some people will believe anything, of course; but it will be increasingly difficult to win widespread credence for ideas that can be scientifically disproven.

It is quite another thing—and wrong—to assert that a new framework of values can only consist of scientifically proven truths. There is a vast portion of life and experience in which science can neither prove nor disprove the truth of assertions. It is in that area that values lie.

The relation of science to our values is not limited to the proof or disproof of assertions. In a brilliant recent essay Caryl Haskins * has pointed out the different consequences for our outlook when we pursue science as a means to power as against its pursuit as a means of understanding. Our avid efforts to "use" science as a means of control have led too often to short-term euphoria as

* Annual Report of the Carnegie Institution of Washington, 1969.

we savored our capacity to exploit and manipulate, but have resulted in ultimate insecurity as we sensed our own inadequacies. In contrast, pursuit of science as a means of understanding moves us toward humility as we are awakened to the intricacy and grandeur of the universe. And it gives us new grounds for a sense of unity with a natural world we once regarded with uncertainty and fear.

That renewed sense of oneness with the natural world, reverent rather than prideful, is reflected in our finally awakened concern for our environment, our renewed concern for all living things and, not least, the future of our species. It is a significant new chapter in man's spiritual wanderings.

THE FIRST STEP

Perhaps the first step toward the reconstruction of personal and social values is the rediscovery of values in one's own tradition. It is a particularly difficult task for the individual who has fought his way out of total imprisonment by his tradition (religious, political, or social). Far from turning to his tradition as a source of spiritual nourishment, he may regard it with cold and contemptuous repudiation. When he looks at it he may find it impossible to see anything but hypocrisies and evasions and fakeries.

But every institutionalized expression of human aspiration shows such stigmata. Ceremonies multiply and ideals thin out. Corruption creeps in. Not all who profess the faith keep the faith. Some exploit the symbols of the faith for selfish purposes. Small wonder that ardent spirits view such compromised institutions with disdain and long to create something new, honest, and uncorrupted. But the new thing they create will also accumulate false fronts and hypocrisies—and quickly. All who profess it will not live by it. So what then? Reject it, too?

The significant question is not *whether* to reject but *what* to reject—and a general answer can be given. It is in the service of life and living values to reject the falsification of values that occurs in any human institution, and to reject those who foster such betrayals of the moving spirit. But rejection is not an end in itself; the end is renewed life—and renewed institutions. It is not in the service of any higher purpose to reject elements in our religious, political, or social traditions that are true and necessary ingredients of the next step in vital belief. In short, in re-examining his own tradition, the individual must look past the flawed surfaces to the often buried elements of truth.

I recognize that it is not easy. The person who is

125

fleeing his own tradition generally finds it more pleasant to dabble in exotic faiths and doctrines. But he will never be at home in those faiths and doctrines. To the extent that he can find a glimmer or grain of truth in his own tradition, it will be a truth that is enriched by early association, a truth that echoes in his memory, a truth that he doesn't have to keep reminding himself is true.

The individual who undertakes the renewal of values today will feel less alone in his arduous task if he acknowledges his kinship with all men and women down the centuries who have sought to create beauty and moral order, whether in religion or politics, art or education, science or law. The honor due them is not diminished by the fact that what they tried to build was betrayed and falsified by others, nor by the fact that what they built was right for their time but not for ours. The structure of values we build today will also outlast its usefulness. But the impulse to build it is sacred.

A SHARED VISION

We need more than individual value systems; we need a shared vision. A nation is held together by shared values, shared beliefs, shared attitudes. That is what enables a people to maintain a cohesive society despite the tensions of daily life. That is what enables them to rise above the conflicts that plague any society. That is what gives a nation its tone, its fiber, its integrity, its moral style, its capacity to endure.

If a society believes in nothing, if it cannot generate a sense of moral purpose, there is no possibility that it will develop the level of motivation essential to renewal.

We will soon begin our third century as a nation. Whether we build in that third century a civilization we can be proud of depends on whether we can arrive at some common conception of what that civilization might stand for, of what it might do superbly well, of what its animating values might be.

We are far from that today. We have a profusion of negative visions—visions of decay, disintegration, sickness, emptiness, failure, and discord. But when we construct positive views of the future they are apt to be the extrapolations of the statistician or the daydreams of the technologist. They lack heart, soul, and guts. They lack the capacity to move us.

Yet our situation is not as bleak as one might think. We do not face the problem of fabricating a new vision out of whole cloth. The exhilarating truth is that the ingredients of the vision are already there to anyone who will open his eyes. They are deep in our tradition and our being; they consist of values we have denied and be-

127

trayed for too long. Young idealists who profess utter emancipation from the past pour out torrents of words about the values they wish to live by, and lo, they turn out to be, for the most part, updated versions of very old values. True, the values have been ignored, traduced, lied about, manipulated, and falsified. But that only says that they need rescuing. And as one repudiates those who lied about the values, one must honor those who lived by them and sought to make them live in our institutions.

In short, we do not come to the task unready. Men and women from the beginning of history have groped and struggled for pieces of the answer. The materials out of which we build the vision will be the moral strivings of the race, today and in the distant past.

The yearnings of the contemporary mind are familiar enough, and I have discussed a number of them in these pages.

We want peace, justice, liberty. We want a society that honors the dignity of each person and proscribes the oppression of one by another.

We seek equal opportunity, equal access to the benefits of the society, an end to the exclusion of some citizens from full sharing in the life of the community. We seek the fulfillment of the individual, the release of human potential.

We believe in individual responsibility and the opportunities for participation that keep responsibility alive. We seek to restore a sense of community and to foster honest, open, and compassionate relations between people.

We seek for each individual the chance to be a whole person, free of the fragmentation that plagues modern life—fragmentation of intellect and emotion, work and play, job and family, man and nature.

We want a society that puts human values above materialism, commercialism, technology, and the success ethic. We seek an end to the dehumanizing aspects of large-scale organization.

We seek an end to the destruction of our natural environment. We want to bring ourselves back into some kind of livable relationship to the animate world of which we are a part and the planet which is our home.

The idea of a society embodying some or all of those values is hardly new. Down the generations, a great many men and women have worked, dreamed, suffered, waited, struggled, and sacrificed to contribute to the grand design of that society. One can see traces of the design in the historical and philosophical writings of the ancient world, in the great religions, in the evolving political thought of the past three centuries.

The idea that man can rationally examine his life, that he need not be the slave of his prejudices, that he can construct a moral framework for living is at least as old as Socrates. It has never been wildly popular. It has suffered long eclipses. But it has always survived, always sprung up again. The contemporary enemies of rationality are not combating a sterile, nineteenth-century, middle-class idea. They are attacking one of the oldest and most stubbornly vital ideas in human history.

The ideas of justice and liberty are not ideas invented by yesterday's liberals, nor by the nineteenth century. They are rooted deep in the history of the race. They have cropped up in one form or another in every great civilization.

It must be emphasized that these moral notions come out of a variety of doctrinal contexts, and people will differ greatly in the religious roots to which they trace the ideas. But the ideas transcend doctrinal boundaries. They have, over the centuries and millennia, had moments of triumph and perhaps more frequent moments of defeat. And even when they triumph, their defenders are human, therefore imperfect, therefore vulnerable to attack by cynics.

Yet the moral ideas will not die. They live. Even in iniquitous times and places they lurk in the minds of men.

VALUES IN ACTION

The identifying of values to which we can all give allegiance is a light preliminary exercise before the

130

real and heroic task, which is to make the values live—
first of all, in one's own mind and heart and behavior,
and, second, in the customs and laws and institutions of
society. The values have been carved on monuments and
spelled out in illuminated manuscripts. We do not need
more of that. They must be made to live in the acts of
men. When ideals are torn loose from the earnest effort to
approximate them, the words swirl endlessly and no one
is enriched, no one bettered, no one saved.

We have in the tradition of this nation a well-tested
framework of values: justice, liberty, equality of opportunity, the worth and dignity of the individual, brother-
hood, individual responsibility. These are all supremely
compatible with social renewal. *Our problem is not to
find better values but to be faithful to those we profess.*
Such values cannot be said to be alive unless they live in
the acts of men. We must build them into our laws and
our institutions and our ways of dealing with one another. We cannot speak of our values apart from the
practical, down-to-earth programs that are necessary to
put them into effect.

If we believe, for example, in individual dignity and
responsibility, then we must do the necessary, sometimes
expensive, often complicated things that will make it
possible for each person to have a decent job if he wants
one. We must provide the kind of education that will enable him to hold a job, the kinds of training necessary for

131

specific lines of work. If he has reached adulthood without learning to read and write, we must offer him basic literacy education. If he has a physical impairment, we must see that he gets medical attention or rehabilitation services. And we must take all necessary measures to insure that there is a job available when he is ready for it.

Similarly, we cannot honestly speak of our concern for individual dignity if we are unwilling to recognize that millions of Americans today are ill housed and that black Americans are barred by discriminatory practices even from much of the housing that is within their reach economically. To correct those circumstances requires federal legislation (which we now have) and federal funds (which we do not have in adequate amounts). It will require changes in building codes, zoning regulations, and labor-union practices. It will require the development of new methods of construction. It will require active participation by the financial community, by real estate operators, by housing developers. It will require action by state legislatures and city councils.

Such complexities take us a long, long way from the lofty phrases about individual dignity, but if we aren't willing to travel that path, the phrases are a mockery.

The translation of our values into social policy has a greater effect on individual morale than is generally recognized. The security and sense of well-being of the individual is directly affected by the extent to which he believes that his society furthers values that seem to him worthy. He wants to believe in his institutions. He doesn't need to believe that his society is perfectly just. But he needs to believe that it strives for justice.

RE-CREATING VALUES

There is no possibility that moral, ethical, or spiritual values can be made to survive from one generation to the next if the only preservatives are words, monuments, rituals, and sacred texts. It is necessary for living men and women to re-create the values for their own time by living the faith, by caring, by doing. That is true of every political faith; it is true of personal ethical codes; it is true of religion.

There is no merit in accepting the faith of one's fathers passively. Faith cannot be a hand-me-down. The religious, political, or social values reflected in any tradition must find new life in response to contemporary needs. This implies an active relationship to one's beliefs. What brings values alive is an attitude in the individual— a commitment, a readiness to act, a willingness to work for realization of the values. That is the heart of a living faith. The way to show reverence for values is

133

to act on them.

Unfortunately, here and around the world, most people still have a wholly passive attitude toward values. The passivity is understandable in historical terms. Until very recently, values were part of the warp and woof of one's tradition. One didn't question; one received. At no time in history was it a healthy attitude; it always contributed to the decay of value systems. But it was the norm.

Today virtually no one feels that he has been handed a complete and coherent set of values that he can accept unreservedly. These days, values come with question marks attached. What is needed is an attitude that accepts what is acceptable from the past, using that as a starting point to build a framework of values for this generation.

Instead of that bracing attitude, we have a continuance into the present of the old, infantile passivity toward values. Contemporary man, his passivity equaled only by his negativism, says, "The faith my father handed me is flawed—therefore I reject it," when he should be saying, "The faith my father handed me is flawed—therefore I have work to do."

Those with a passive attitude toward values regard a "faith" as something that relieves them of responsibility and makes further seeking and striving unnecessary. If they accept the faith of their fathers, they do so unquestioningly and their spiritual life is over before it begins. If they reject that faith, they seek a substitute that they can swallow whole. When such individuals talk of their search for "meaning" or "faith" or "something to believe in" one gets the impression that they conceive the object of their search as a kind of wonderful secret room they will someday stumble into. Once they find it the struggle will be over. No more effort. No more doubt. No more striving. So they try a lot of rooms. Zen Buddhism? Drugs? The latest political "religion"? But they never find the wonderful place where effort ceases, because it doesn't exist short of the tomb.

What does exist—if they will shift their attitude from passive to active—is a chance to *create* meaning in their lives. It is a building process and it is never finished and the rewards are in the doing. Faith is a building process, acting to bring vitality to one's faith.

The individual who has accepted the necessity for a positive and active attitude toward the renewal of values will be better prepared for the deep frustrations of that task. He will not let those frustrations induce discouragement or cynicism or spasms of self-pity. And he will see that to serve his values is to make them real in everyday life—in his own behavior and in his community.

The latter task poses particularly difficult questions

135

today. Most of our institutions are so intricately organized that few understand how or why they work. If a huge and impersonal institution functions in such a way that some people suffer an injustice, who is to blame?

One of the most common phenomena of modern life is the sight of a man of the highest personal values presiding over an institution that mocks those values. Fifty years ago Lincoln Steffens noted that some of the most evil political machines he encountered were presided over by men of rather high personal moral standards. Similarly today the television network that merchandises violence may be presided over by a man who personally abhors violence, and the industrial company that spews pollutants into the city's air and water may be run by a man who wouldn't drop a chewing-gum wrapper on the sidewalk.

Men who preside over institutions must accept some personal responsibility for the undesirable consequences of institutional action. I hasten to say that this does not mean dissociating oneself from imperfect institutions. That is a popular course today, and it is usually wrong. The task of those who care the most is to get in and change the institution for the better.

But the individual—especially the young person— who is trying to get his own values straight had better begin by concentrating on values that have consequences

136

in his own behavior. He must test *his own* values in action. The task of sitting in judgment on huge institutions is easy, but invites a moral righteousness that the individual may not apply to his own acts. One should prepare for moral judgments about others by exercising an unsparing moral judgment on oneself.

It can be a revealing exercise. The moral duplicity of large institutions is notable, but the flaw is in the species before it is in institutions. *As individuals,* we have a gift for professing much and delivering little, for mouthing the words and not living by them. And the man who speaks most fervently against such duplicity may be one of the worst offenders. The run-of-the-mill hypocrite may deceive others; the one who believes he is free of hypocrisy deceives himself.

CHAPTER EIGHT

We Still Have a Choice

The mode through which the inevitable comes to pass is effort.

—Justice Holmes

I F YOU ASK someone to describe his idea of Utopia, the chances are he will outline a world that is at odds with everything we know about man and his institutions. He will ignore (or deal unrealistically with) the flaws in human nature that every society must cope with continuously. He will ignore the tendencies in human organization that will always imperil individuality. But his most important omission will be the element of moral striving.

138

Typically, his Utopia will be static. Perfection will have been achieved. And much that makes life alive will thereby have been eliminated. There is no seeking when you have already found; no problem-solving when you have the answers; no joy of the climb when you're sitting at the summit; no thrill of cultivation when it's always harvest time. Such perpetual success without effort, arrival without journeying, solution without trial and error would be inanimate—and insupportably dull. It is precisely that inanimate quality, the absence of any element of effort, that makes the conventional concept of "happiness" so bland, empty, and meaningless.

We are not at our best when the battle is won; we are strivers, at our best when the goal seems nearly unattainable. That is our nature. And it fits us well for the world in which we find ourselves. There are inescapable features of the human condition that guarantee the continued struggle.

There are things in human nature that make static perfection unthinkable. For example, if we could today completely eliminate from the society all prejudice, all hostility, all tyrannizing of one man over another, it would begin to creep back tomorrow. And there are things in human organization that make static perfection impossible. If we could bring our society to a pitch of perfect vitality and creativity today, the processes of decay would begin tomorrow. The tendencies of human organization to rigidify, to exalt form over spirit, to stifle individual creativity, to resist innovation would reassert themselves—and if not countered would eventually triumph.

The truth is that we can look forward to no rest. We can seek and find; but what we find today will be taken for granted—or rejected—tomorrow. And the search will begin anew. We can prove the great theorems today, but new theorems will take their place. The moral insights of tomorrow will make today's striving seem primitive.

That is living, and we are well fitted for it.

WHAT CAN ONE MAN DO?

Even the alert, informed, exceptional American is farther down the path to the beehive model, more securely "locked in" to a specialist role in the society than he realizes. He is more awed, more cowed by the overarching systems that govern our lives than he would be willing to admit. The whole style of modern social organization erodes his sense of responsibility, particularly as regards social action. It tells him in a thousand ways, "You aren't important. What you do won't make a difference. It's not up to you anyway." So he works within the lines of his specialty, plays his highly defined role, and hopes that somehow everything will come out all right. Everyone has noted the passivity that results. The passivity is intensified by the deeply ingrained spectator and consumer habits of modern man.

In the abstract, there is no correct answer to the question "What can one man do?" If any substantial number continue to believe that one man can do a great deal, then they will preserve a system that sustains their belief. But if the overwhelming majority believes that the correct answer is "nothing," then the system will become one that confirms that answer. The danger lies in a downward spiral—diminishing confidence on the part of the individual that he can possibly affect the system; therefore necessarily more paternalism on the part of the system; consequently even less initiative on the part of the individual, and so on. At the bottom of that downward spiral will lie the wreckage and the memory of a free society.

We shall not get through our troubles safely until a considerable number of Americans acknowledge that they themselves are part of the process by which the society will be made whole.

For those who are honestly concerned to solve the problems of this society, there is hope. There is a road that leads on to a better future. It is the path of tough-minded analysis and action in behalf of social change,

141

the path of hard-driving, patient-impatient pressure to redesign our institutions, to educate our people to a changing world, and to cope with the hatred and anger in our hearts.

It is the path chosen by the individual who has committed himself to the fight for a better future and is strong enough to face the frustràtions of bringing about real social change.

He does not waste time looking for scapegoats. He does not indulge in moral posturing. He does not entertain the mind-poisoning conviction that all the nation's difficulties stem from the actions of people morally less worthy than himself. He does not imagine that the main point is to show how angry he is. Nor will he yield to the joys of self-exoneration; he will acknowledge that he himself may have contributed to our troubles.

He works for change at the same time that he works to preserve the continuities without which society would fly apart. Thus he may work for fundamental revisions in the criminal justice system at the same time that he fights to preserve continuity in the tradition of due process. He knows that human institutions require both needling and nurture.

He carries on an unending two-front war—on the one hand against extremists who would destroy the system, and on the other against the deadly combination of selfishness and apathy that blocks significant social change in this country today.

He knows that freedom and order are inseparable, that coercion in the cause you agree with paves the way for coercion in the cause of whoever controls the instruments of oppression.

He may even have that rarest of qualities today—a touch of humility. We have lived with a kind of adolescent pride for so long that we are deeply suspicious of the very idea of humility. We have believed that man could achieve anything. We have believed that this nation could accomplish anything it set out to accomplish. We have glossed over our limitations, puffed ourselves up, denied the tragic flaws in our character. And that too is a kind of hypocrisy. We will not be lesser men if we admit our common humanity. We are not gods. We know so little, have so many bad habits, preen ourselves so ridiculously on small victories. For the sake of our dignity, a little humility is in order.

TASKS FOR THE TOUGH-MINDED

There is heavy work ahead, work for able and courageous men and women who are willing to tackle the evils of the day in a problem-solving mood. We have plenty of provocateurs, plenty of people who treat public affairs as an opportunity for personal catharsis or glorification. We don't have plenty of problem-solvers.

As a people we have a considerable gift for not being honest about our problems. We can look directly at them and deny that they exist, or deny that they're serious, or deny that money need be spent to solve them. And those are forms of frivolity we can no longer afford.

We shall accomplish none of the significant tasks if we count our short-term comfort as more important than our long-term future, if we are unwilling to tax ourselves, if we lack the courage to demand disciplined behavior of ourselves and others.

We will not accomplish the exceedingly difficult tasks of redesign that lie ahead without a combination of commitment and cool intellect. Intellect alone won't generate the courage and determination necessary to cut through the obstacles. But the contemporary fashion of ardor without intellect is even more inadequate. Accomplishing social change is a task for the tough-minded and competent.

We tend to think of the social and moral order as one might think of a house that someone else built—static and completed, something one could live in for a long time without renovation. But the social and moral order is more closely akin to an individual's physical balance,

144

which is the product of the countless nerve and muscle reactions that maintain it. Consciously or unconsciously, the individual is working on it every waking moment; if the effort ceases, he collapses.

So it is with the social and moral order. It is an ever-changing product of all the acts that bear upon it, some of them disintegrative, some regenerative.

As a people, we still have a choice. If we want a society on the beehive model, all we need do is relax and we'll drift into it. If we want a society built around the creative possibilities of the self-directing individual, then we have tasks to perform.

Each of us has tasks to perform. Each of us is that self-directing individual. This free society begins with us. It mustn't end with us.

APPENDIX

What to Do About
the Cities

I DO NOT spend my days on the large abstractions covered in the body of this book; I work on concrete social problems—housing, voter registration, the delivery of health services, and all the other substantive issues of urban life. Questions of action are uppermost—how to obtain suitable federal legislation on urban problems, how to persuade leaders in a particular city to face up to racial tensions before they explode, how to bring police, courts, and correctional institutions into mutually reinforcing collaboration, and so on.

I would find it hard to end the book without reference to that level of activity, not simply because it occupies so much of my life but because the reader will grasp more clearly the larger issues covered in the book if he has the concrete problems vividly in mind.

No matter how fervent our professed allegiance to social objectives, nothing will happen unless citizens care
enough to act. Formally the system asks only that we
enter the polling booth periodically and register our
choices. But we cannot expect significant social change
unless many of us take a deeper and more continuous interest. We must monitor the actions of public servants,
carry on tasks of public education, man the party machinery, lobby in the public interest, and honor leaders
who lead. Effective action requires organized effort, attention to detail, and staying power. It also requires a
close grasp of issues. In what follows, I shall try to provide an introductory sketch of one set of public issues—
those surrounding the urban crisis.

Many people are deeply concerned about the cities
without having the faintest idea what the urban agenda
is. Too many Americans have come to equate the crisis
in the cities with racial tensions, and they are tired of the
race problem and wish it would go away. It won't go
away, but if it did, the urban crisis would remain. Discrimination, in some measure, touches most urban issues
in this country. But such critically important issues as
housing, manpower, and income for the poor deeply involve white as well as black. Most of the poor are white.
And one cannot blame racial tensions for our monumen-

tal traffic jams, for the inexorable advance of air and water pollution, for the breakdown in administration of the courts, for the shocking inefficiency and often corruption of municipal government.

Make no mistake about it, the urban crisis is a major crisis in the management of complexity and change. It is true that when urban systems malfunction, minorities and the poor are hit first and hardest, but the problem is deeper and broader and ultimately affects us all.

If middle-class Americans imagine that by moving to the suburbs they can leave the pathologies of the city behind them, they are wrong. The health of the society is indivisible. When we allow social ills to spread through any segment of the community, the whole society suffers.

Quite aside from questions of moral concern, we have a gigantic investment in our cities—in physical plant alone—and cannot turn our backs on it. The cost of social disintegration is very great; when it occurs in a neighborhood, that area becomes a burden on the taxpayers not only in the rest of the city but in the state and the nation. When a child develops a lasting physical handicap through lack of early medical attention, he often becomes a lifelong burden on the rest of the community.

It is not possible to quarantine serious social pathologies. Crime and the drug traffic may thrive first

149

in areas of social breakdown, but eventually they spread to other areas. The tensions and anger generated in one segment of the society affect the whole tone of our national life.

In short, we pay—in taxes, in social disorder, in rising crime rates, in a diminished sense of well-being, and most of all perhaps in the growing awareness that our system has failed some of our citizens.

To meet the urban crisis will require action on many specific problems—education, the administration of justice, and so on—but it will also require changes in three major systems: the collection and distribution of public monies, the structure of government at all levels, and present patterns of land use and population deployment. I shall begin with these major systems.

MONEY

It will take a lot of money to cope with the urban crisis, and the cities themselves cannot supply it. The central city is staggering under a rapidly increasing burden of expenditures for education, welfare, sanitation, and law enforcement at the same time that its tax base is eroding.

150

Some cities might conceivably raise slightly more money through new kinds of taxes or through users' charges. And municipal borrowing could be made a more fruitful and dependable source of funds, particularly if the idea of an Urban Development Bank were adopted. But the main source of additional funds is likely to be the federal government.

Some people have observed with disappointment the apparently modest results of multibillion-dollar federal programs and have concluded that, in tackling our social problems, money isn't the answer. It is true that money alone isn't the answer. Discussing this subject, a friend of mine said recently, "I have great skepticism as to what can be done with money." I told him it was matched by my skepticism as to what can be done without money. In most areas of federal action, *money must be combined with significant strategies for renovating inadequate institutional arrangements.*

Where will the money come from?

The first requirement is a healthy economy, and all appropriate measures to that end are directly relevant. Beyond that, leaders must have the courage to propose —and citizens the vision to support—appropriate tax measures. Place such a recommendation before any practical politician, now or five years from now, and he

151

will say, "Correct, but now is not the time." It never is.

We must tax ourselves to deal with what ails us. It is absurd for the fattest, richest nation on earth to assert that it can't afford to cope with the problems that are tearing at its vitals. We can't indulge in such hypocrisy and continue to respect ourselves. According to the most recent available comparisons (1966), of all the world's major industrial powers only Japan ranked below us in total taxes as a percentage of gross national product.

Tax reduction has an almost irresistible appeal to the politician, and it is no doubt also gratifying to the citizen. It means more dollars in his pocket, dollars that he can spend if inflation doesn't consume them first. But dollars in his pocket won't buy him clean streets or an adequate police force or good schools or clean air and water. Handing money back to the private sector in tax cuts and starving the public sector is a formula for producing richer and richer consumers in filthier and filthier communities. If we stick to that formula we shall end up in affluent misery.

Is it not possible that the sovereign citizen would understand those simple facts if his leaders had the guts to tell him? Perhaps he doesn't really want to end up as Croesus on a garbage heap.

At least as important as adequate taxation is action to

152

correct the inequities in our tax laws. If the American people are to bear the costs of essential urban programs through federal taxes, then they must have confidence that the tax system is equitable. The tax-reform legislation passed by Congress in 1969 left the job half done.

Given the great difficulty of raising taxes, we must reorder national priorities on the expenditure side. There are many ways in which money may be saved, if anyone has the political courage to do it. Farm price and income supports, highways, and the projects of the Bureau of Reclamation and the Corps of Engineers cost us many billions a year. One could list other expenditures that at the very least deserve searching reappraisal in the light of desperately important priorities of the moment.

But the part of the budget that most urgently calls for scrutiny is the defense budget. At this writing defense expenditures stand at about 44 per cent of total federal expenditures. Yet there is still no adequate national debate or review procedure governing either our overseas commitments or our military budget.

The domestic departments exercise a considerable measure of discipline over their expenditures, not because they are thrifty by nature—far from it—but because they are subject to tough, raking scrutiny by the Bureau of the Budget and the committees of Congress. If that scrutiny were eliminated, they would grow lax and fat. That, in a nutshell, is the condition that has prevailed in the defense establishment for many years. Recently we have seen for the first time in many years a willingness on the part of both Congress and the public to face the problem. What is needed, on a continuing basis, is an unsparing examination of every aspect of defense spending, an examination that will extend to procurement practices, use of manpower, administrative overhead, maintenance of overseas bases, and the basic rationale underlying force levels and weapons systems.

Now let us suppose we have succeeded in the difficult but essential reordering of priorities and have some money to spend. Some of that money will flow into the city in very indirect ways (for example, in incentives and subsidies to stimulate private-sector housing efforts). Some of it will flow in through state, county, or federally administered programs. And some of it must go to the municipal government itself in the form of revenue sharing. In addition, it may be necessary for the federal government to accept total responsibility for funding one or another of the major functions of local government (probably welfare).

In federal categorical assistance—that is, grant programs for specifically defined purposes—there must be a consolidation and simplification of grant categories to reduce the enormous number of present programs.

The states can assist the cities by picking up a substantially greater share (maybe all) of the cost of elementary and secondary education, and by picking up part of the bill for mass transit and other urban development expenditures. To be able to give such assistance, every state must make an adequate tax effort (both income and sales taxes). The federal government could hasten that day by providing an income-tax credit that would benefit states to the extent that they tax themselves.

GOVERNMENTAL MACHINERY

If the first thing we need to solve the problems of the city is money, the second is improved governmental organization at every level. I discussed some aspects of the problem in Chapter Five.

In matters of government, one must think in terms of metropolitan, state, and regional patterns and not just about the central city. For many the word urban has come to mean only the central city, and that is a hopelessly constricted view of the problem.

In Chapter Five we examined some of the shortcomings of government at the local level. It is astonishing that this society, which creates such extraordinarily efficient organizations to serve certain of its purposes, such as space exploration and merchandising, tolerates an incredible slovenliness in the structure by which it governs itself. I'm not speaking of the necessary untidiness of self-government. I'm speaking of structural weaknesses that every informed witness has inveighed against for years.

Of course, some citizens believe that weak government isn't a bad thing. But weak government (local, state, or federal) doesn't mean that no one is in charge. It does mean that the people aren't in charge. Often it means that special interests are profiting considerably by keeping government weak.

Any attempt to strengthen local government must look first to the states. The cities are creatures of the state, and many of their troubles stem from failures of omission or commission on the part of the state. It is particularly important that the states re-examine and, where appropriate, ease legal barriers to adequate local taxation, and that they liberalize controls over borrowing by local government. The states should allow local governments to determine their own internal structure, subject only to broad requirements.

The states can also do a good deal to combat the incredible fragmentation of local government. There are 119 municipalities in Cook County, Illinois, for example, most of them very small. Roughly half of the 5,000 municipalities in the major metropolitan areas * are less than one square mile in area. Two-thirds of them have fewer than 5,000 inhabitants, one-third have fewer than 1,000.

The splintered jurisdictions fragment the tax base, prevent economies of scale in local government, and stand in the way of any national policy for the total metropolitan area. One or another form of metropolitan-area government is desirable but the political obstacles are great and there is much that can be done short of that goal. The states should ease present restrictions on annexation so that cities could absorb nonviable units on their borders, and they should set standards for the incorporation of new local governments within the metropolitan area to halt proliferation of small, nonviable units. It might be useful to create metropolitan area commissions to review new applications for incorporation and recommend consolidation where desirable.

States should re-examine all of their support formulas for local government and revise them in such a way as to create incentives to consolidate units of local government. The federal government should do the same. In many states today, state-aid formulas function as incen-

* Specifically, the Standard Metropolitan Statistical Areas defined by the Census Bureau.

tives to maintain many small units of government.

State and federal agencies should also eliminate policies that lead to the proliferation of special districts and should substitute, where feasible, policies that strengthen general, multipurpose government.

At the same time that they are combating the senseless fragmentation of local government, major cities and urban counties must seek to revive neighborhoods and to create neighborhood subunits of government. This is *not* senseless fragmentation. It need not diminish the power of the city or county to cope with the problems that cut across jurisdictions.

In order to accomplish all the necessary tasks, some states may have to amend their constitutions. Every state should create a department of urban affairs (twenty states have already done so) which could formulate urban policy and administer financial and technical assistance to metropolitan areas in planning local government organization, building code modernization, and so on.

And state legislatures must be greatly strengthened and must meet annually, and legislators must be adequately compensated and staffed.

The federal government can also assist greatly in strengthening local government through revenue sharing, through consolidation of categorical grant systems, and in many other ways.

158

PATTERNS OF HUMAN SETTLEMENT

At the national level the paralyzing effect of fragmentation may be seen in our failure to think clearly about patterns of human settlement and population movement. Those problems have been neglected in part because they cut across the jurisdictions not only of local governments but of most of the domestic departments of the federal government.

Federal agencies have always made decisions (consciously or not) that sharply affected patterns of human settlement and population movement. In recent years such decisions have been made by the Federal Housing Administration, by the highway program, by the Department of Defense in awarding defense contracts, by all agencies in deciding on the location of major installations around the country. And those unwitting policy decisions were often sharply at odds with other federal actions which consciously sought to bring order out of urban chaos—for example, efforts to encourage area-wide planning requirements, to strengthen regional bodies, and to rehabilitate the cities themselves.

Everyone now recognizes that a long-term solution for the cities must reach beyond the cities themselves. Much

159

of urban poverty is rural poverty recently transplanted. The heavy migration of the rural poor to the inner cities has created enormous social dislocation. Quite aside from such migrations, we face a major problem in the very large population increase anticipated between now and the year 2000. If we are to accommodate the increase we shall have to think flexibly and imaginatively about how we can best use the land space of the nation. What patterns of settlement and open space best serve our purposes? How can we revitalize rural areas, create new cities, and overhaul existing cities in ways that serve human needs, the requirements of economic vitality, and the claims of beauty?

The National Committee on Urban Growth Policy has recommended creation of a hundred new cities averaging 100,000 in population and ten new cities averaging one million in population. If anyone asks what American industry can possibly do without the stimulus of war and an arms race, that recommendation is one possible answer. One hundred and ten new cities! Cities, I would specify, that relegate to history the outworn nonsense of residential segregation; cities that are fit places for young people to grow up in and for older people to live out their lives in dignity; cities that in every respect are designed for

160

people.

Many urban affairs experts have been put off by uto-
pian descriptions of the gleaming new city arising far
from the mess of existing metropolitan centers. They find
in such writings a millennialism, an antiseptic city-plan-
ner zeal, and an unseemly eagerness to turn one's back
on existing troubles. As a matter of fact, it would be a
grave mistake to launch a huge national effort confined
to new cities. We need a program that links the building
of new and satellite cities, the rebuilding of old cities, the
planned expansion of existing small cities, and rural economic development.

Such tasks pose a challenge worthy of the best that is
in us. Such efforts would generate vast new economic activity. They would create jobs. They would provide the
dynamic thrust that our society has always had in the
past and is in some danger of losing.

If we allow the present disastrous conditions to persist,
they will grow worse as the future unfolds. The cities
aren't going through a temporary disorder. Even if the
migration of rural poor into the central city ceases, the
natural population increase will bring greater and greater
congestion to the ghetto. There is no present evidence
that the cities can reverse, or even stem, the flight of industry to the metropolitan fringe, taking jobs and poten-

161

tial taxes with it. Deserted by the middle class, ringed by the discriminatory zoning of suburbs, its physical plant decaying, the central city will become increasingly an enclave for the aged, the poor, and victims of discrimination.

What steps can be taken to achieve a better outcome?

The federal government should consider providing financial incentives for state and local action; capital grants and low-interest loans for advance land acquisition; incentives to business and industry to locate in areas where growth is sought; and incentives and assistance to people in moving from labor-surplus to labor-shortage areas.

The states, with federal help, could create new statewide agencies with broad powers to plan new communities, to establish urban development corporations, and to create "land banks." States should also use their full authority to locate highways, air terminals, parks, hospitals, and universities in such a way as to implement a statewide plan for land use and population movement.

A compelling argument is made by some experts that a federal grants-in-aid approach would produce no coherent result and that what we need is a powerful federal instrumentality such as NASA or a federal-regional instrumentality such as TVA to plan and carry through the desired program as regional economic development.

So much for general considerations. Before turning to the specific, substantive problems of the city, let me say a word about the interlocking problems of poverty and race. Neither appears as a separate category in the following pages because each breaks down into components that must be dealt with in its own right.

A successful program for coping with poverty must include attention to sound management of the economy and to economic growth. It must include a fully developed manpower strategy, including full employment, job training, and equal opportunity. It calls for adequate programs of income maintenance—unemployment insurance, Social Security, public assistance. It requires rehabilitation of the victims of poverty and elimination of the urban and rural slums where poverty is bred. To help the individual we must have programs of education, health care, and social services. To change the environment we need massive urban rebuilding, broader than anything conceived to date, as well as regional and rural economic development.

Similarly, any approach to the problems of race must soon move beyond large, vague assertions concerning

163

racism to specific programs. The problems of blacks, Mexican-Americans, Puerto Ricans, and other minorities are ultimately problems of housing, employment, education, health, income maintenance, and so on. We shall deal directly with those components.

I shall not repeat in each of the following sections what must be obvious to everyone who has observed the urban crisis: that while we must discuss the problems in technical terms, what is ultimately at stake in every case is human suffering, shocking disparities in individual opportunity, and the anger and tension of frustrated citizens.

HOUSING

The Housing Act of 1968 established a ten-year goal of 26 million units, 6 million of them for low- and moderate-income families. The act recognized that the goal could not be achieved without mobilization of private sector resources; it made some—though perhaps not adequate—provision for the subsidies and incentives without which private enterprise cannot play its part.

At this writing, there is serious doubt that the goal set forth in the act will be achieved. The obstacles are formidable. The most serious obstacles at this writing are the interest rate and the shortage of mortgage financing. Beyond that, we must find ways to produce housing more efficiently, and that depends on our capacity to assemble markets sufficiently large to permit economies of scale. The aggregating of markets depends in turn on our capacity to break through multiple archaic building codes and restrictive zoning.

The existing stock of inner-city housing is deteriorating with frightening speed, leading to the abandonment of many dwelling units because rents are not high enough to allow owners to maintain the property. Only federal help can enable the cities to arrest this decay, and to turn it into an opportunity to rebuild core areas over the next generation. Some effort in this direction has already been made; more is necessary.

Restrictive zoning is another serious obstacle to achieving an adequate volume of low- and moderate-income housing. In the New York metropolitan area, less than 1 per cent of the undeveloped land zoned for residential use is zoned for multifamily dwellings. The suburbs have found that zoning is an effective method of economic and racial discrimination. The states have the power to place limits on the abuse of zoning powers but they are unlikely to act unless the federal government creates incentives to do so.

Another constraint is the spectacular rise in land costs.

165

To ensure the availability of land for low- and moderate-income housing it is essential to extend and enlarge the federal advance land-acquisition program, increasing greatly the funds available for the purpose of "land banking."

At the same time the federal government must assist the states to move toward metropolitan areawide agencies and statewide agencies with the authority to proceed in the acquisition of land and development of housing for low- and middle-income families.

A major effort is needed to overcome discrimination in housing, but it *must* be linked to efforts to increase the supply. Sheer unavailability of low-income housing (for blacks *or* whites) is the primary problem today.

EMPLOYMENT

We have created an incredible tangle of federal employment programs, and we must move soon to untangle them. We need to combine current manpower efforts into an effective and integrated program.

We must improve vocational training. It is frequently unsuited to the job opportunities available in a given locality and often neglects the basic reading, writing, and arithmetical skills so essential to job marketability.

166

We must find ways to encourage and stimulate industry to do more in job creation, in removing racial barriers, in hiring hard-core unemployed, and in training and upgrading on the job. But the problem cannot be solved fast enough by private employment alone. Only a program of public-service employment will produce jobs in sufficient volume and with the speed the urban crisis demands. Such a program should be specifically designed to avoid make-work projects and dead-end jobs. The hard-core unemployed need work that will add to their capability and broaden their opportunities to become productive members of the work force. Basic education, training, and counseling must be an integral part of the program.

Training and upgrading opportunities should be available to all who wish them throughout the work force. It is estimated that skill upgrading is essential for roughly 10 per cent of the work force, and our present manpower-development efforts reach approximately 1 per cent. Until we do better than that we shall continue to live with the contradiction of large numbers of unemployed people and a vast unmet need for trained workers in an expanding economy.

Finally, in many cities there is a serious problem of relating jobs to people geographically. In some cases it is a question of providing mass transportation to get people to their jobs. In other cases it is essential to enable the

167

poor to move to where the jobs are—which means a head-on attack on racial barriers. In still other areas it may be desirable to encourage industrial location in the inner city.

EDUCATION

Either through increased funding of the Elementary and Secondary Education Act, earmarking of shared revenues, or assumption by state governments of the local burden of school financing, we must get more money into the cities for education. The schools, like the cities, are going broke. It is of special importance that we channel funds to schools in low-income areas that need the money most desperately. Title I of the Elementary and Secondary Education Act was designed for that purpose but has fallen grievously short of the goal.

Dependence on the property tax for school financing means that districts with high numbers of low income families will have less money to spend on education than will economically secure (i.e., suburban) communities. In other words, "them as has, gits." State aid to education frequently discriminates against urban areas by allocating more money per pupil to suburban and rural areas than to inner-city areas. That is hard to believe but it is true. Those who seek reform have brought suit in a

168

number of jurisdictions to prove that state financing procedures result in systematic and injurious discrimination against some classes of individuals.

We must continue the difficult but necessary effort to desegregate the schools, and we must resolve the conflict between those who seek and those who oppose community control of schools. The brawling fight on this subject in New York City has convinced many that it is a virtually unsolvable problem, but a number of cities are moving toward one or another form of community control without major conflict. It is not easy, but it can be done.

We must continue to experiment with methods of teaching disadvantaged children. We have seen less than a decade of intensive work on the subject, and we have a lot to learn.

Finally, we must press ahead with the development of assessment procedures that will enable us to measure the successes and failures of the schools. There can be little effective accountability of the schools to the citizen as long as there are no measures of performance.

INCOME FOR THE POOR

All efforts to help the poor are hampered by the myth that the poverty population is made up chiefly of able-bodied loafers. The facts disprove the myth. Of

169

the 25 million poor in the year 1968, more than one-third lived in families in which the family head worked full time but still couldn't make enough to climb out of poverty. As the President's Commission on Income Maintenance Programs pointed out, if the head of a family of four worked forty hours a week, fifty-two weeks a year, at the minimum wage of $1.60 an hour, family income would still fall below the poverty level. And there are at least 10 million jobs in this country, including some in state and local government, that pay less than the federal minimum wage.

Another third, roughly, of the 25 million poor in the year 1968 lived in families where the family head had only a part-time job, either because it was seasonal or because full-time work was unavailable.

In other words, the great majority of family heads among the poor have demonstrated their willingness to work, and what they need are decent, full-time jobs at wages that will lift them above the poverty level. In some cases they first need the training that will fit them to hold such jobs.

There remain approximately a third of the poor who are not working at all and require cash income assistance. Most of them are too old, too young, or too handicapped physically to enter the job market or are mothers who cannot leave their children to go to work. A

170

relatively small number (estimates vary from 50,000 to 150,000) are able-bodied males, and many of those would work if jobs were available and if they had the skills to qualify.

The failings of the present welfare system are familiar: grossly inadequate benefit levels in most states; absence of provisions for the working poor; lack of adequate work incentives; provisions in half the states that encourage the breakup of families; a patchwork of federal, state, and local eligibility requirements that leave many without assistance altogether.

We cannot continue with that system. Rather than argue the details of various proposals now under debate, let us ask ourselves what a workable system must include. We need an income-maintenance system covering all the poor; full federal financing and administration of the system; benefit levels at the poverty line; uniform eligibility standards; and work incentives.

Before leaving the subject, let us remind ourselves of what may or may not be expected from a welfare program. Much of the poverty that makes such a program necessary is rooted in inadequate education, insufficient job opportunities in the locality, discrimination, the pathology of the urban and rural slum, low pay in jobs not covered by the minimum wage, inadequate social-insurance benefits, inadequate provisions for manpower train-

171

ing, and so on. No welfare program can cure those underlying conditions; it can only deal humanely with the consequences. If we are to get to the root of the problem we shall also have to take vigorous action in education, health, and nutrition programs, the creation of job opportunities, the elimination of slum conditions, and similar measures. In addition, we must increase Social Security benefits and experiment with new methods of providing supportive services to welfare recipients.

HEALTH

Arrangements for delivering medical care are increasingly costly, badly distributed, and unsatisfactory. Many people are hard pressed to pay for the care that is available, and others—notably the poor—find that services are simply not available. Among the problems are obsolete and decaying facilities, shortages of health manpower, and the gross inefficiency of the existing health machinery—inefficient methods of practice, wasteful use of highly skilled professionals, lack of effective control on expenditures, and duplication of effort. The problems are made worse by lack of unified federal policy and direction in the multiplicity of government-supported programs.

172

We can improve health care for the poor by redesigning present methods of delivering health services. We can improve the manpower supply through training programs to make available more of the traditional as well as new types of health workers. We can stimulate prepaid group practice, which has been demonstrated to have a beneficial influence on the productivity of health services as well as on cost control. But none of these objectives will be achieved without major alterations in professional and institutional attitudes and practices. The rigidities of the present system constitute the major obstacle.

The provision of adequate family-planning services and adequate public education with respect to those services is a major responsibility of the health professions, and they have yet to put their full energies into that task.

In our concern for the delivery of health services, we must not diminish the support of biomedical research. In the long run, research may do as much as all our more "practical" efforts to improve the health of the poor.

MINORITY ECONOMIC DEVELOPMENT

Those Americans who object to unconventional tactics on the part of minority groups seeking power had better think about how to give minorities a

173

share of conventional power.

Politically that means access to the ballot, so long denied to black citizens in the South, and access to the party machinery. Economically it means expanded opportunities for individuals as owners, managers, and employees.

Efforts to provide jobs—and upward mobility in jobs —have been numerous; we've been at that task a long time and know what must be done. The effort to provide minority-group members with opportunities as owners and managers is newer. When the idea first became popular in 1968–69 it suffered from early excesses of enthusiasm, and from some early failures. Federal leadership was notably uneven, and the most dedicated proponents of the idea differed sharply among themselves as to what constituted sound doctrine.

No one disagrees, however, that financing is a key to all of the various proposed solutions. A good many qualified experts have urged formation of a national development corporation that would finance minority economic projects in somewhat the same way as overseas projects are financed by the World Bank and similar bodies.

And no one really disagrees that technical assistance is a key element in any solution. One solution would be for the Small Business Administration and other federal agencies to earmark a percentage of their funds for tech-

174

nical assistance to minority entrepreneurs.

There are other aspects of the problem that deserve early and systematic attention: how to test various patterns of community ownership, how to insure sheltered markets, and so on.

One problem is that too many of the efforts toward minority economic development end up encouraging black people to get into independent small businesses. And small business is a hazardous enterprise today, whatever the color of the owner's skin.

LAW ENFORCEMENT AND THE ADMINISTRATION OF JUSTICE

Nothing will more surely convince the citizen that his society has failed him than a breakdown in justice and order, yet our arrangements for law enforcement and the administration of justice are in disarray. We all suffer the consequences, whatever our income level, but the poor suffer most acutely the frustrations of a faulty system—inadequate protection, inadequate representation, delays, and inefficiencies.

Much that is wrong with the criminal justice system today could be corrected through internal reorganization, the introduction of modern management tech-

niques, better recruitment, training, and personnel procedures, and more adequate funding. The police need
career development programs, community relations
training, and better pay. The lower state and local
courts, underfunded and manned by ill-trained and over-
worked personnel, are poorly fitted to dispense justice.
Interminable delays are only the most visible evidence of
organizational breakdown.

Means must be found to deal with the huge volume of
cases that clog the system but are not, strictly speaking,
matters of criminal justice—traffic violators, alcoholics,
narcotics addicts, and so on. It is possible, for example,
that an agency patterned after the National Labor Relations Board could be created to handle all routine land-
lord-tenant conflicts.

Juvenile court procedures still fall far short of providing the required constitutional guarantees. The probation
system in nearly every city is overburdened to the point
of being nonfunctional. Detention facilities are over-
crowded and lack educational or counseling programs.
The widely shared view that except in serious crimes first
offenders should be kept out of correctional institutions
—even, if possible, out of the courts—is rarely practica-
ble because of the lack of organized alternatives, for example, provisions for counseling and job placement.

There must be some means of planning that covers all
elements of the criminal-justice system. Such a means

176

has been tested in New York City in the Criminal Justice Coordinating Council, which combines in a single planning body, under the strong leadership of the mayor, representatives of both public and private interests concerned with the effective functioning of the system. Mayors and leading citizens in every city should press for the establishment of such a council.

In those parts of the city that have a high incidence of poverty, excessive rates of teen-age unemployment and other symptoms of social disintegration, crime is of course part of the general pathology and won't be cleared up until the underlying conditions are corrected. Crime is inextricably linked, for example, with addiction to hard narcotics, and unless we learn to cope with the latter we shall never cope successfully with the former.

All public agencies must be accountable to their constituencies and responsive to the concerns of the citizen. In the inner city the police must be in touch with the people and responsive to their anxieties; in most cities this will require the establishment of communication channels that do not now exist.

THE ENVIRONMENT

We are making wholly inadequate progress—in some respects we are losing ground—in environmental pollution control. We now know that the advocates of pollution control who were counted as alarmists ten years ago, even five years ago, were in fact underestimating the complexity and danger of the problem. We are farther along the road to disaster than anyone had thought.

We must not only control known contaminants of our air, water, and land but develop the means to anticipate new hazards. We are doing neither. Federal efforts to control air and water pollution have been a miserable failure.

Except for human waste discharged into water, pollution is overwhelmingly an industrial problem. There are many nonindustrial sources of pollution, but, in general, pollution is (and is perceived as) a head-on conflict between industry and the convenience of the citizen. Anyone who has watched the conflict over the past ten years must be impressed by the steady rise in public anger; no sensible businessman can fail to be concerned about the deepening of that conflict. But few business leaders have been courageous or even candid in fighting for pollution control. What should we expect of them?

Above all, they should take the hard but necessary steps, in collaboration with government, to make pollution control an accepted part of the cost of doing business. The governmental role is crucial. No one firm can afford the added cost if its competitors are evading it.

178

And effective governmental regulation cannot occur until industry ceases its highly successful efforts to emasculate pollution control legislation. Pollution control technology is developing rapidly and will move even more rapidly if tough legislation, vigorously enforced, creates a real market for it.

We need new patterns of collaboration that we do not now have. If a river is to be cleaned up, it must involve the collaboration of many industrial installations and many municipalities. None can do the job alone. Again, the role of government is crucial.

Public opinion may ultimately be the most powerful weapon in behalf of pollution control. The industrial executive insists that the sidewalk in front of his company's headquarters be swept clean, while at the other end of town his smokestacks belch filth. He believes the public will judge him harshly for the cleanliness of his sidewalks but that it is not yet sophisticated enough to judge him by his smokestacks. But the public is learning.

Automobiles present a special problem. There is at this writing no viable alternative to the internal-combustion engine. That engine can be cleaned up considerably, but the enormous projected increase in the number of autos will more than outweigh the reduction in pollution by each individual vehicle. It may prove necessary to adopt one of the rather severe measures under discussion

179

—for example, barring private automobiles from the central city or levying a steeply graduated tax on horsepower that would get us out of our big gasoline-eaters into smaller cars.

CONSUMER PROTECTION

Consumer protection covers a broad range of topics, from gas pipeline safety to auto insurance abuses, from radiation protection to home improvement frauds. Consumer protection laws must be extended to cover all relevant products. Today we have an illogical patchwork of coverage. We cover medicines but not medical devices, power mowers but not death-dealing toys. There are grave inadequacies in consumer protection in fields of vital interest to the poor, particularly food and credit.

A more effective federal role in consumer protection will require improved organizational arrangements within the Executive Branch, including a strengthened co-ordinating unit in the Office of the President and a well-staffed, well-funded "consumer's lawyer" with ample investigative powers to represent the consumer before federal agencies and in judicial proceedings. It will also require a complete overhaul of the Federal Trade Commission and major strengthening of the Food and Drug

180

Administration. The Department of Agriculture must be forced by public opinion and by Congress to act more aggressively in consumer protection—a difficult goal given its long ties to producers. In all relevant departments there must be much more research on harmful ingredients and nutritional values.

The basic consumer right—adequate information on which to base judgment—requires research on product safety and efficacy, honest labeling, full disclosure of all relevant information by sellers. A number of people have advocated a federally supported semi-independent National Consumer Information Foundation to meet the need for research, testing, and standard-setting. Departments that now do extensive product testing (chiefly the Department of Defense and the General Services Administration) should be required to release results to the public.

Vigorous federal antitrust action can get at not only price fixing but collusive efforts to block product innovation.

Finally, there must be an intensified effort to right the imbalance between buyer and seller in the courts. It is not only that the seller has ample funds and a high-priced lawyer; it is that generations of such lawyers have brought to a high state of development those aspects of the law that protect the seller and creditor. Too little at-

181

tention has been given the remedies available to buyers and debtors.

In our efforts to strengthen the executive branch, we must never forget that even the ideal agency will look bad if Congress writes weak laws, prescribes weak penalties, denies the agency adequate powers, and deliberately introduces complications and delays into the enforcement process. Workable enforcement procedures and rigorous penalties are essential. We need a broad new consumer protection law that will proscribe a clearly defined set of frauds and deceptions. And we need legislation permitting consumers to bring class suits to recover damages.

Some of the most significant advances in consumer protection have come from Congress, but some of the cleverest efforts to weaken consumer legislation have come from the same source. With the latter in mind, James Goddard, former Commissioner of the Food and Drug Administration, has urged that members of Congress be required to make full public disclosure of their business, professional, and financial interests.

TRANSPORTATION

Over the past two decades most cities have switched from primary dependence on public mass

182

transit to predominant use of the private automobile. Yet during those same two decades the cities have experienced a huge influx of poor people who must depend wholly on mass transit. This new pattern is a grave handicap to all who do not use automobiles, not only the poor but the aged and the handicapped.

Present sources of funding insure that the imbalance will continue; federal funds are available more readily and on more favorable terms for freeways than for mass transit.

None of the ills of mass transit will be solved until we find better means of financing. The cities, with their limited capacity to raise money through taxes, are simply unable to foot the bill. Federal grants for capital investment should be tripled. A good many experts believe that we need a Mass Transit Trust Fund comparable to the Highway Trust Fund. It would help if some way were found to capture in taxes even a tiny fraction of the enormous appreciation in land values that results from public investment in transportation facilities.

Public mass transit has suffered from a lack of innovation, particularly in technology, perhaps, but also in the way it is operated and organized. The federal government should sponsor research and development in all aspects of mass transit.

Patterns of transportation determine to a considerable degree the patterns of city living. That is why transporta-

183

tion planning must go hand in hand with other aspects of community life and growth (placement of sewer and water facilities, schools, hospitals, business districts, low-income housing, and so on). It is essential, for example, that the jobs and housing available to the urban poor be linked by mass-transit facilities.

Unfortunately, sensible transportation planning is almost impossible, given the present fragmentation of interests. At the federal level better coordination must occur among the Departments of Labor, Transportation, and Housing and Urban Development, particularly with respect to the transportation of the poor. Locally, the fragmentation is not just the familiar geographical splintering into multiple jurisdictions but a splintering by mode of transport. We must soon have metropolitan or regional agencies empowered to plan and act for all modes of transportation.

This Appendix has dealt with far too many subjects too rapidly, but it was my purpose to give the reader a glimpse of the full range of urban questions and a sense of the complexity of those questions. Each of the questions deserves a full-length book in its own right—a task which I happily leave to other authors.

184

Index

Action, reflection and, 98–102
Agenda, the, 22–23
Allen, James, 17
Automobile pollution, 179–80

Bible, 18
Bureau of Reclamation, 153
Burke, Edmund, 22

Carnegie Institution of Wash-
    ington, Annual Report of
    (1969), 123
Change, continuity and, 31–32
Cities, concern about, 147–84
    administration of justice,
        175–77
    consumer protection, 180–
        82

education, 168–69
employment, 166–68
environment, 177–80
governmental   machinery,
    155–58
health care, 172–73
housing conditions, 164–66
income for the poor, 169–72
law enforcement, 175–77
minority economic develop-
    ment, 173–75
money and, 150–55
patterns of human settle-
    ment, 159–64
transportation, 182–84
Coercion, violence and, 48–51
Common purpose, leadership
    and, 83–102
    binding element in pluralism,
        85–88

Common purpose (Cont.)
  contemporary leadership, 95–98
  government, 88–91
  public and private sectors, 93–95
  reflection and action, 98–102
Community, individuality and
  opportunity to serve, 76–77
  participation, 72–74
  quality of life, 74–76
  repair of fragmentation, 78–79
  self-discipline, 79–82
Confidence, erosion of, 51–52
Consumer protection, 180–82
Continuity, change and, 31–32
Continuous renewal, 33–34
Cook County, Illinois, 156–57
Corps of Engineers, 153
Criminal Justice Coordinating
  Council (New York City), 177
Criminal-justice system, 175–77
Criticism versus contempt, 106–8

De Maistre, Joseph Marie, 83
Discrimination, housing, 132, 166
Dissent, 35–53
  defense of status quo, 38–
42, 52, 53
  and revolution, 42–45
  erosion of confidence, 51–52
  extremists and majority, 46–48, 52–53
  interplay and, 52–53
  leadership and, 108–12
  politics of provocation, 45–46
  violence and coercion, 48–51
Dropout, defined, 63

Economic development, cities
  and, 173–75
Education, 168–69
Elementary and Secondary Education Act, 168
Employment, cities and, 166–68
Environment, city, 177–80
Equal opportunity, goal of, 61–62
Excellence (Gardner), 60
Extremists, the majority and, 46–48, 52–53

Federal Housing Administration, 159
Federal Trade Commission, 180
Food and Drug Administration, 180–81

Fragmentation, repair of, 78–79

Goddard, James, 182
Government
 common purpose and leadership, 88–91
 machinery, 155–58

Harrington, Michael, 106
Haskins, Caryl, 123–24
Hazlitt, William, 119
Health care, 172–73
Holmes, Oliver Wendell, 138
Hope, self-contempt and, 103–18
 criticism versus contempt, 106–8
 dissent and leadership, 108–12
 expectations and performance, 104–6
 myth of regress, 112–14
 optimism, 116–18
Hostility to institutions, 26–31
Housing Act of 1968, 164
Housing conditions, 164–66
 discrimination, 132, 166
 restrictive zoning, 165
Human settlement, patterns of, 159–64
Hypocrisy, 137

Income for the poor, 169–72
Individual, society and, 54–64, 138–45
 internal communication, 58–60
 moral, 62–64
 pluralism, 54–58
 release of individual potentialities, 60–62
 tasks to perform, 138–45
Individuality, community and, 65–82
 opportunity to serve, 76–77
 participation, 72–74
 quality of life, 74–76
 repair of fragmentation, 78–79
 self-discipline, 79–82
Institutions, redesign of, 17–34
 the agenda, 22–23
 continuity and change, 31–32
 continuous renewal, 33–34
 hostility to institutions, 26–31
 problem solving, 23–26
 self-examination, 19–22
Internal communication, 58–60

Jeffers, Robinson, 54
Justice, concern about, 175–77

Law enforcement, cities and, 175–77

Leadership
  binding element in pluralism, 85–88
  common purpose and, 83–102
  contemporary common-purpose difficulties, 95–98
  and dissent, 108–12
  government, 88–91
  public and private sectors, 91–93
  reflection and action, 98–102

McCarthy, Joseph, 52
Marcuse, Herbert, 47–48
Military-industrial complex, 55
Milton, John, 100–1
Money, city crisis and, 150–55
Morale, 62–64
Municipalities, 156–57
Murray, H. A., 65

Nader, Ralph, 106
National Aeronautics and Space Administration (NASA), 162
National Committee on Urban Growth Policy, 160
National Consumer Information Foundation, 181

National Labor Relations Board, 176
No Easy Victories (Gardner), 98

Ombudsman idea, 42
Opportunity to serve, community and, 76–77

Participation, community, 72–74
Peace Corps, 71, 77
Pluralism, 54–58
  binding element in, 85–88
  meaning of, 55
Pollution control, 177–80
  automobiles and, 179–80
Population increase, 160
Potentiality, release of, 60–62
President's Commission on Income Maintenance Programs, 170
Problem solving, 23–26
Provocation, politics of, 45–46
Public-private collaboration, 91–93

Quality of life, individuality and, 74–76

Reflection and action, 98–102
Regress, myth of, 112–14
Revolution, dissent and, 42–45

Self-contempt, hope and, 103–18
  criticism versus contempt, 106–8
  dissent and leadership, 108–12
  expectations and performance, 104–6
  myth of regress, 112–14
  optimism, 116–18
Self-discipline, 79–82
Self-examination, 19–22
Self-exoneration, 20
  self-pity and, 114–16
Self-Renewal (Gardner), 25
Shared vision, 126–30
Sinclair, Upton, 106
Slavery, 61
Small Business Administration, 174
Social Security benefits, 172
Society, individual and, 54–64, 138–45
  internal communication, 58–60
  moral, 62–64
  pluralism, 54–58
  release of individual potentialities, 60–62

tasks to perform, 138–45
Status quo, defense of, 38–42, 52, 53
Steffens, Lincoln, 106, 136

Tennessee Valley Authority (TVA), 163
Tradition, 124–26
Transportation, city, 182–84

U.S. Department of Agriculture, 181
U.S. Department of Defense, 159, 181
U.S. Department of Labor, 184
Urban crisis, 147–84
Urban Development Bank, idea of, 151

Values, renewal of, 119–37
  in action, 130–33
  in one's own tradition, 124–26
  internal gyroscope and, 120–24
  re-creating, 133–37
  shared vision, 126–30
Violence, coercion and, 48–51
Volunteers in Service to America (VISTA), 77

Whitehead, Alfred North, 35